MJ Magazine

VOLUME I • ISSUE 3

The Magazine Created by Authors for Authors

Fran Lewis, Founder

PUBLISHED BY FIDELI PUBLISHING INC.

ISBN: 978-1-60414-798-9

Fideli Publishing Inc.
119 W. Morgan St.
Martinsville, IN 46151

www.FideliPublishing.com

Cover image: Can Stock Photo Inc. / HaywireMedia

Dedicated to Marcia Joyce with love from Frani.

Table of Contents

Book of the Month

Recommended Reading

Fran's Top 5 New Authors

Featured Romance

What's Your Opinion?

Books Dealing with Issues

Issues: Bullying

Issues: Medical Concerns

Dellani's Stories

Enrico's Bakery – Hartsdale

Address: 214 East Hartsdale Ave., Hartsdale, NY 10530
Hours: 6:30 am - 8:00 pm
Phone: 914-723 0340
Owner: Joseph Floriano

Gennaro's Pizza

Address: 759 Central Park Ave, Scarsdale NY 10583
Phone: (914) 472-6329
Owner: John

Go Greenly

Now open in Scarsdale serving: Fat Free Fresh Frozen Yogurt, the Best Smoothies in Westchester. Banana/Pineapple and Blueberry/Banana are the best! There are so many choices, frozen yogurts and toppings. It is a yogurt lover's haven for healthy treats.

Address: 1088 Central Ave. Scarsdale, NY 10583
Phone: (914) 713 8693

Hartsdale Hair Studio

Address: 4 E. Hartsdale Ave., Hartsdale, NY 10530
Hours: Mon - Sat - 9:00am - 6:00pm Sunday's 10:00am - 2:00pm By Appointment
Owner: Evelyn
Phone: 914-437-7811

Luigi of Italy

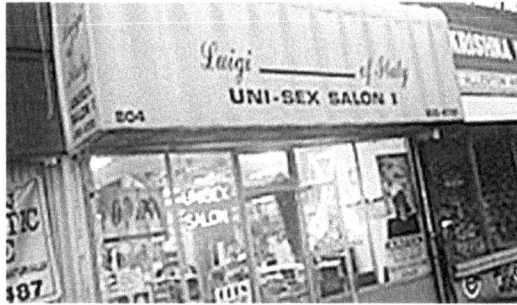

Address: 804 Allerton Ave, Bronx, NY 10467
Phone:(718) 655-4700
Owner: Tony

Remembering Marcia Joyce

Fran Lewis

Every morning at exactly 7 a.m., my sister would call me on my cell phone. She thought I needed a morning wakeup call, even though I did not. Her special way of saying hello—elongating the first part—was hysterical. She would start with, "Hell-lo, sister dear. Are we in a good mood or a bad mood today? Do I need to cheer you up or can we get on with our morning conversation? Did you have your caffeine or should I wait until you walk to the bakery and bring back breakfast for everyone?"

Then she would go on with her instructions for the day. "Mom needs a new chair, a new vacuum cleaner, and some more wipes." The wipes and the supplies were ordered from a homecare place and they handled that, but the rest I told her would wait until she arrived for one of her visits. Of course, it would mean doing some research on vacuums and lift chairs for the best prices. The lift chair we were able to get from a contact that she made working for doctors. The other was my job to research, so I did. I went to the sources that would help me, and I don't mean Google search. I talked to Mom's home health aides, who advised me to get a Dirt Devil, which was easy to use and required little maintenance. I listened to them because I wasn't doing the vacuuming, they were.

My sister would then proceed to tell me about her upcoming vacation plans, her visits to my nieces, and all about the parties that I couldn't attend because I was caring for Mom. It became a joke after a while—"I get to go and you get to not go."

Last year my niece, Dani, my sister's daughter, turned sixteen, and I represented the family at her party in Florida. I just wish my sister could've been there so I could say, "I finally got to go! What do ya think of that?"

My sister was a ball of energy and never ceased to amaze me. She was a fireball and never got tired of dancing, reading, going out, and having fun. The thought of spending a quiet evening on the weekend at home was unheard of for her unless she was sick. She loved life and she loved people. Most of all, she loved her family and we loved her.

Miss you always, sister dear,
Frani

MORE MEMORIES OF MARCIA ...

Marcia Wallach...what a very special lady! I was fortunate to have her as my boss for nine wonderful years at an orthopedic office. She was more than a boss; she was like a sister and best friend. Working at the office with Marcia was such a pleasure. Even though it was an office, she made it feel like we were part of a special family.

She was such an understanding person. If ever a problem arose, Marcia was always there to help—be it in the office or on a personal level. She always took the time to listen and advise. Marcia had a saying, "*Don't sweat the small stuff.*" Every time I feel stressed, I can hear her saying these words in my ear.

I can remember holidays at the office with Marcia at the helm. On Halloween, for example, we would dress up in costume for the patients, as well as our-selves. Everyone would come in costume. We always had such fun! Photos were always taken and are treasured forever. I am so thankful we have those photos!

She was a beautiful person inside and out. She was also a loving sister, wife, mother, and grandmother, always talking about her children, grandchildren, and family. She was so proud of them all!

I will always remember my boss and friend Marcia Wallach. Marcia taught me a lot of things for which I am forever grateful. She will forever live in my heart. No one can ever replace Marcia as my office manager because she was one of a kind, as well as a friend.

—Judy Scarpella

THE SEARCH FOR RESEARCH

R.J. Ellory

"No matter what you do, no matter how hard you try, you can never escape your own memories...."

I stand quietly ahead of a small, industrial lake. It is a cold January morning in Washington D.C. Beside me stands a man I have spent merely a day with, a man who has driven me around his city to show me scenes of some of the worst killings he has ever investigated. His name is Brad Garrett. He is known by his colleagues in the Federal Bureau of Investigation as "Doctor Death." During his twenty-five-year career in the DC area, no homicide has taken place that has not engaged his professional attention. He has no children; he and his wife do not share a surname. Very few people know where they live, and his neighbors are not aware of what he does for a living. This is the way his life has to be.

The remark he made, the comment regarding never being able to escape his own memories, was in reference to a case that still wakes him in the cool, semi-darkness of early morning, a case that still haunts him without respite or relief.

"There isn't a day that goes by when I do not think about it," he adds quietly.

The case of which he speaks is very disturbing.

A fisherman, casting lines out into that small, industrial lake, saw a thirty-gallon trash can float to the surface of the water. The lid, once wired to the can itself, had come loose, and in the can he could see two heads. The police were called, and once the can was dragged onto land it was discovered that a Vietnamese woman and her two-year-old child, both kidnapped some five months earlier, were inside the can. From all appearances it seemed that they had been tied together and put into the can alive, face-to-face. No one was ever arrested for the crime. No one has ever been questioned. No one knows what happened, and—more than likely—no one ever will.

Earlier that day Brad had taken me to a branch of Starbuck's where three young and innocent workers were murdered in a failed late-night robbery. There was a memorial to the three dead kids, and part of that memorial was a series of three boxes, within which could be found small mementoes placed there by family members. That case was Brad's first active DC murder investigation after an earlier, lengthy case which had seen him tracking a known terrorist and murderer out of the US into the Middle East, arresting that terrorist, smuggling him back into the US under the very noses of that Middle Eastern government, and securing his charge, arraignment, trial, conviction, and execution. That terrorist had assassinated three active CIA operatives on US soil and then fled justice.

Before even that we had spoken of his work on the infamous Washington Sniper case.

3

Brad Garrett was a quiet and methodical man. He talked, but he did not talk easily. His responses to my questions were measured and precise, as if he was always aware of what he was saying…careful to say enough, but never too much. But it seemed he enjoyed speaking of his career, his life, his "passion for the truth." He knew that his career had become an addiction, a word he used himself, and he knew that he would never escape the need to know what was behind the scenes, what was on the other side of the crime scene tape. He had seen the worst that the world had to offer, and yet kept coming back for more.

I left Brad Garrett by the side of that lake in Washington, D.C., and drove up into Virginia. I entered a town called Falls Church in Fairfax County, and there I met a woman called June Boyle. June was a thirteen-year veteran homicide detective, her years before homicide having been spent in robbery, sex-crimes, and many other areas, and alongside Brad Garrett she had been one of the lead investigators in that very same Washington Sniper case. June was immediately charming, very warm, very human, and she drove us to a park where we sat on benches near a snow-covered playground and spoke of her life in the police department. The surroundings were surreal, but the conversation was very real indeed.

The Washington or "Beltway Sniper" case was the most important investigation on the east coast for as many years as anyone could remember. Events transpired during three weeks in October of 2002 that resulted in the deaths of ten people, the critical injury of three others, and the collective inhabitants of Washington, Maryland and Virginia enduring a reign of fear the like of which they had never been experienced before, and would be unlikely to ever experience again.

Without any understandable rationale or motive, John Allen Muhammad, 41, and Lee Boyd Malvo, 17, went on a killing spree, travelling in a blue 1990 Chevrolet Caprice Sedan, into the trunk of which a

hole had been bored, and through that hole — employing a stolen Bushmaster XM-15 semi-automatic .223-caliber rifle — they had fired upon innocent citizens. A landscape gardener, a retired carpenter, a babysitter, a woman vacuuming her car in a gas station, a thirteen-year-old on the way to school…Muhammad and Malvo shot these people from a range of fifty to one hundred yards. At such a short distance, a .223 caliber bullet does a remarkable amount of damage to the human body.

Detective June Boyle was the detective who finally interviewed and secured a confession from Lee Boyd Malvo, the younger of the assassins. She spent six and a half hours with him. She secured his confidence and his trust. She arranged his food, she sent out for veggie burgers, for boxes of raisins, at one point sitting with a handful of raisins as he took them one by one and ate them. She got him to open up, to really start talking, and with that information the case had a foundation and a grounding that would never have been possible without her. Despite the fact that the attorney general authorized Malvo's trial to take place in Virginia, and thus gave the jury the opportunity to execute him, the jury decided not to. They gave Malvo life in prison. I asked June how she felt about this, and in a split second the warm and forgiving appearance vanished, within a heartbeat the humor and humanity was gone, and she said, matter-of-factly, that Malvo should be dead.

"There are some people in this world that should be dead," she continued. "Lee Boyd Malvo is one of them."

It was a glimpse behind the face that she wore for the world. In that moment I realized that despite her generosity of spirit, despite the fact that she was a tremendously big-hearted person, she was also a police detective, and had been witness to some of the very worst kind of people the world had to offer.

"This is a lifestyle, a vocation, something that you can never leave behind," she told me. "When I am away from it, even though it is terrible, I still miss the rush, the excitement, the buzz of a new case, a new lead, the feeling that it was going somewhere…"

At one point towards the end of our discussion she showed me two cellphones, one from her left coat pocket, one from her right.

"This one," she said, holding out the phone in her right hand, "is my personal phone. I might as well leave it at home. It never rings. No one ever calls me."

She paused and smiled wryly.

"But this one," she said, holding out her left hand, "is my work phone. It rings all the time, and every time it rings there's a dead person at the other end. It could be a domestic abuse case where the wife has finally tied of her husband's cheating and put a kitchen knife through his heart. It could be a gangland killing. It could be a hit and run. It could be a twelve year-old girl in pieces in a dumpster behind a derelict hotel. I never know what I will find, but it is always bad. Just when you think people have done the very worst that they can to one another, you find someone has gone and done something even more terrible. There is no limit to the imaginative ideas applied to the destruction of other human beings."

This is a reality that is hard to face, and yet is a profound and disturbing truth. With Brad, with June, there is an intensity, a passion, a need to see what further darkness lies behind the façade of society. Where any "normal" person would shy away from looking, such people as these look harder. But who is the more "normal" —those who seek the truth, or those who evade it? I believe, perhaps, that Brad and June are at the very least fully apprised of what men and women are capable of doing to one another, and thus are not overwhelmed by it. They also appreciate and accept that such individuals—the ones who shoot and stab, those who strangle and mutilate others—are in the tiny minority. It has been said that that which you can face will never become your master. Perhaps, in seek-

ing the most fear-inducing realities of existence, they have become—to some degree—fearless.

But both of them speak of their lives like there was no choice for them. This was something they had to do. Never a matter of if, but when.

Later, interviews complete, alone in a hotel room in a strange city three and a half thousand miles from home, I contemplate my own place in all of this. I am the journalist, the spectator, the voyeur, the eyewitness to all of this. This, a country I was not born in, and yet choose to write about. I will always be a tourist, nothing more nor less. I am a stranger in a strange land, and yet I am also compelled to dig deeper, to look beyond the façade, to find what lies beneath.

Paul Auster said that becoming a writer was not a "career decision." You didn't choose it so much as get chosen, and once you accepted the fact that you were not fit for anything else, you had to be prepared to walk a long, hard road for the rest of your days. I concur with his viewpoint. I am compelled to do this, incomparable perhaps to the work of people like Brad Garrett and June Boyle, but still a compulsion. I have no choice. I have to ask. I have to step closer. I have to look, and then look again. I have to remember what I asked, what was said in response, what I felt, what I perceived, and from this I have to create my own realities, my own universe, my own cast of characters who will walk in those spaces where people fear to go.

Sometimes my wife stops me working, if only for a little while.

"You are too intense, too involved," she says. "I know you have to be, I know that this is the way you are, but every once in a while you need to let go. Take a walk; come spend some time with the family. Have a rest from the terrible, terrible people you seem so devoted to spending your time with…"

And she is right. Of course she is right.

I walk away, just for a little while, a few hours perhaps, but I can never really let go. I want to hear from Brad Garrett's own lips how it was to find the dead woman and her child in the trashcan. I want to hear June Boyle tell me again what it felt like to look into the eyes of a man who had just woken on the morning of his own execution. I want to see what they saw. I want to feel what they felt. I want to know so I can write about it, share it with others, evoke emotions, capture attention. Why, I do not know. Why do any of us do the things we do. Because we have to? Perhaps. I am not concerned with the answer to that question. My interest lies elsewhere.

I spent a week in Washington, D.C., capital of one of the richest and most powerful nations in the world. But the criminals there are just the same as everywhere else. The killings are just as pointless. The lives wasted are no more valuable than anywhere else on the planet.

I spend a few of my final hours in this city in the company of Alyce. Alyce is thirty-one, a mother of two. Her son is nine and lives with his grandma. Alyce's daughter, getting on for three years of age, lives with Alyce. I am not going to give you Alyce's surname or the names of her children for obvious reasons. Alyce, for ten years, was a heroin addict. She was homeless, destitute, broke, and a junkie. At one moment I asked after the whereabouts of her daughter's father. "Well, he lives in the same doorway where I used to live…."

Alyce has just finished the third year of her medical studies. She has been off heroin for a little longer than that. She has another two years to go, and when she graduates as a nurse she wants to specialize in helping those who are adversely affected by drugs. She has recovered her relationship with her parents and her siblings. She has secured low-income housing and lives in a really nice house (because she has made it so), and she is testament to the fact that people can survive.

Alyce is generous, warm, friendly, talkative, very open about her life and her personal experiences, and she has an optimistic outlook for the future. I ask her about Obama, the possible changes, the political and cultural future of America, and she smiles wryly. She says, "Race doesn't matter. Doesn't matter what color the president is. He seems to be a smart man. The last one wasn't smart. That's the thing that will make a difference." A very astute observation. While the rest of the world is talking about what color the president is, someone right there in the middle of it sees it for what it is. Is he smart, or is he dumb? That's the thing that will make a difference.

It is my last full day in the US capital, and though I had accomplished what I set out to do, I also felt that I had looked through a window into something that would have ordinarily been unattainable. Tourists don't get into the Washington Post, they don't talk to FBI agents or homicide detectives, they don't walk through low-income housing complexes and speak with recovered heroin addicts about the trials and tribulations of being sick and poor and a parent. Yet somehow they possess a strength of spirit sufficient not only to survive those experiences, but to then dedicate the rest of their lives to helping people escape from the same terrible circumstances.

On Sunday morning, I went out to Columbia Street. I stood on the street where Catherine Sheridan was murdered at the start of *A Simple Act of Violence*.

In a strange way this was more sobering than anything else.

I write fiction. I create characters and put them in fabricated circumstances, and whether I write for the sake of entertainment, or I write to evoke an emotion, or I write simply for pleasure, I am still writing fiction.

Standing there on Columbia Street and thinking about Catherine Sheridan, so soon after having spoken to Brad Garrett about the Vietnamese woman and her baby, after having spent time with June Boyle and listening to her talk of the Washington Sniper case, the arrest and interrogation of Lee Boyd Malvo, the fact that the jury saw pictures of his victims, innocent people with their heads blown apart, and then were confronted with pictures of Malvo as a baby and were sufficiently influenced on a sympathetic level to over-turn the death penalty...standing on that street and talking about a fictional character made me so much more aware of the real people. The ones that do die. The ones that are murdered. Sobering, to say the least.

I took a great deal of memories away from Washington. I think they are things that will stay with me for the rest of my life, and will certainly inform and influence my writing.

I am so often asked why I write about America. I am often challenged, accused of trying to be something I am not.

I disagree. I tell stories. That's what I do. I have always done this, and I believe I always will. I feel I have a duty and a responsibility to engage and inform and educate and entertain. I believe that there are things I can show people that they otherwise would never see. I believe this is a privilege, and it is something that I feel very fortunate to do.

I am one of life's travellers. I go there, I look, I see, I report back. I try to bring home the emotion, at least that if nothing else.

I am trying to live as many lives as I can within a single lifetime, and some of those lives are filled with darkness, and some are not.

Each is important as the next. This is something I cannot escape, just like Brad Garrett cannot escape his memories.

———

R.J. Ellory is the author of *Three Days in Chicagoland*, which focuses on the brutal murder of a young girl in Chicago in 1956, as told from three different viewpoints: The Sister, The Cop and The Killer. His other books are *Candlemoth, Ghostheart, A Quiet Vendetta, City of Lies, A Quiet Belief in Angels, A Simple Act of Violence, The Anniversary Man, Saints of New York, Bad Signs, A Dark and Broken Heart, The Devil and the River.*

CONTEXT DOES NOT COVER A MULTITUDE OF GRAMMATICAL SINS

David Workman

A friend of mine who knows my propensity for being a Grammar Nazi constantly argues that the context of a phrase or sentence makes up for poor grammar, excusing it because the context allows the reader to still understand what is being said even if the grammar isn't perfect. At face value, that argument seems to make a great deal of sense. After all, the whole point of language is to communicate information in a manner that the recipient understands what is being said and can act on it. Good enough, right?

Nope. Not buyin' it. And here's why....

We've all heard the principle that "love covers a multitude of sins." That's actually Biblical, from I Peter 4:8. At the risk of starting a theological debate (I do love a good one, but just not here), does that ideal pertain to grammar sins? Is context the language equivalent to love? Does it cover a multitude of grammatical guffaws? Or is it a classic case of the Bible being taken out of, well, context and used to serve one's personal agenda? I'd say we go with that one.

While love may cover the sins and forgive the sinner, context does not justify bad grammar. Misspellings, poor punctuation, and split infinitives are still wrong. In fact, they make reading harder because the reader first stumbles over the poor grammar, causing disruption to the flow, and then has to rewind and read it again so context can try (sometimes in vain) to clean up the mess. This is not why context exists. In fact, I would argue this relationship between context and grammar is completely reversed.

Context and grammar do play well together, and the burden of clarity falls solely on context's shoulders to tell grammar what to do. But that doesn't mean

> College admission tests should include using your, you're, then, than, their, there and they're correctly in sentences.
>
> If you fail, you must restart the 4th grade.

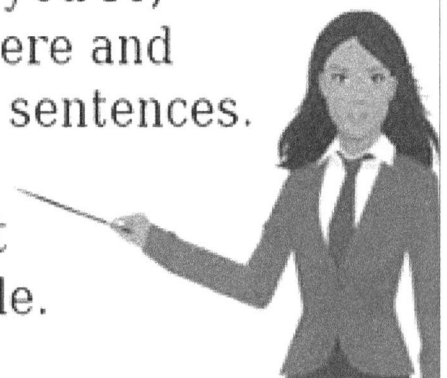

8

context is always the boss. Take the classic case of there, their, and they're. Which one do you use? That depends on the context. If the context dictates they're and you write there instead, it's still wrong even if the reader can figure out what you meant to say. In this case, context doesn't help; it only serves to make the grammatical error even more glaring.

Or how about a dangling participle? (So embarrassing in public!) Sure, the context will probably help you figure out what it's supposed to modify, but why make the reader work that hard? Why not just do it right in the first place?

Is context important? Yes. Is proper grammar important? It's vital. Does context cover a multitude of grammatical sins? No.

Relying on context for clarity is a pitiful excuse for grammatical laziness. Bad grammar is still bad grammar! Fix it and the reader won't have to struggle through your writing.

David Workman's debut novel, *Absolute Authority,* hit the shelves in early 2012 to roaring acclaim. A native St. Louisan, he was recently named by local television station KMOV as one of St. Louis' Top 5 New Authors. Along with writing novels, David has spent most of his 20-year writing career hammering out advertising and marketing copy for companies large and small, including his current gig as the lead contest specialist for a major athletic shoe company. His second novel, a sequel, is scheduled for a winter 2013 release. Find him on Facebook.

THE TIMES THEY ARE A-CHANGIN'

Robin Surface, president, Fideli Publishing Inc.

Amazon's worldwide dominance has changed nearly all the rules when it comes to books and book selling, and because it posted $61 billion in sales last year, publishers and authors have to pay attention. Self-published authors especially need to switch gears and start thinking about how their books will look when presented online. This means paying attention to book cover design and being aware of what viewing your cover at thumbnail size does to its design.

Let's deal with the typography first. The book's title should be big and easy to read, the subtitle should be legible and the author's name should be big enough to read when the cover is at thumbnail size. Remember, nearly all of your potential customers are viewing your book online. If your cover looks like a blurry blob when viewed as a thumbnail, it's not doing a good job of enticing potential buyers.

Because the size of the thumbnail image is so small, simplicity is the best way to go. If you try to show everything that goes on in the book on your cover, you're going to end up with a mess. Your cover is intended to provide *some* information about the contents of the book as well as portray an overall feel for the subject matter. That doesn't mean including images of all the characters; a lot of what is communicated by the cover is done through styling, color, and typography.

Take a look at the cover below to see what happens when you try to put too many elements into this small space. It looks like a bunch of unrelated images and to top it off, you can't read the subtitle because it gets lost in the background and the author's name is tiny. Do you think this cover motivates potential readers to buy? It would probably have been better to use the Raven as the only image, since the subtitle includes the text "Soaring Raven."

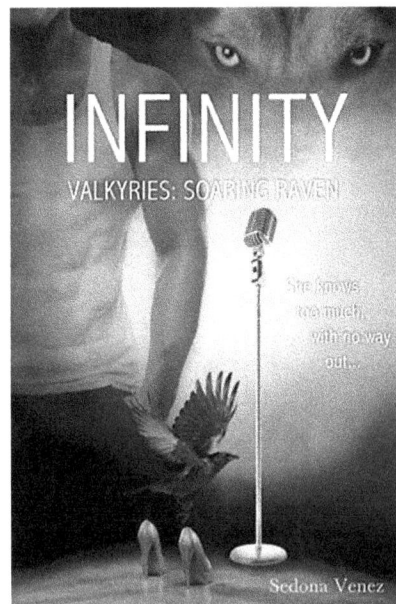

I know everyone has his or her opinion about the subject matter of the *Fifty Shades of Grey* trilogy, but I personally think the book covers are genius. As you

10

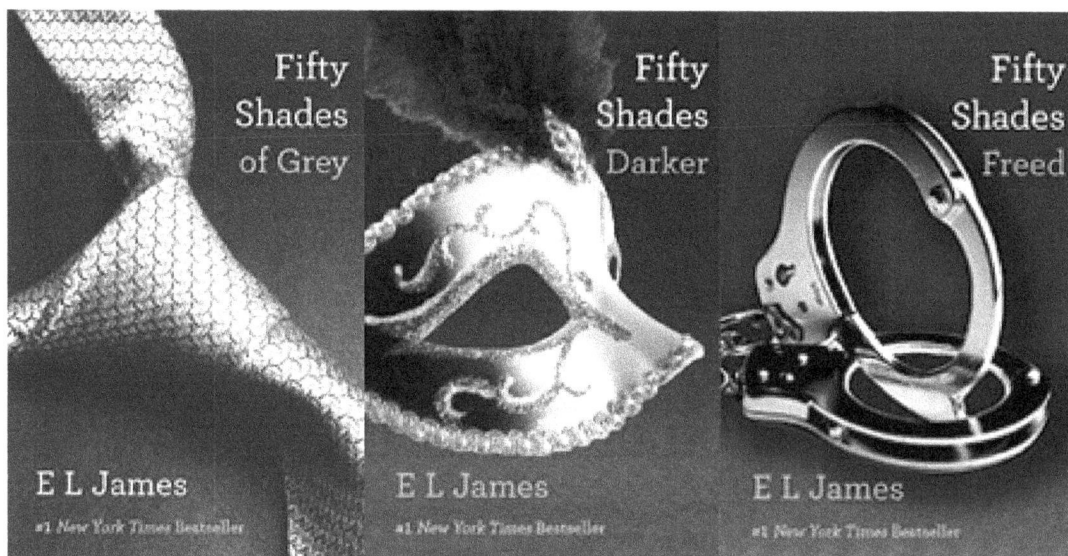

can see above, each cover uses one image in a large size to create a nice effect. The background sticks to only shades of gray in keeping with the title. Notice that you can read both the title and the author's name even at this reduced size.

want to know more. Do you think you or I would have the same reaction to a cover that showed, say, Main Street of a small town with the title and author's name?

Probably not.

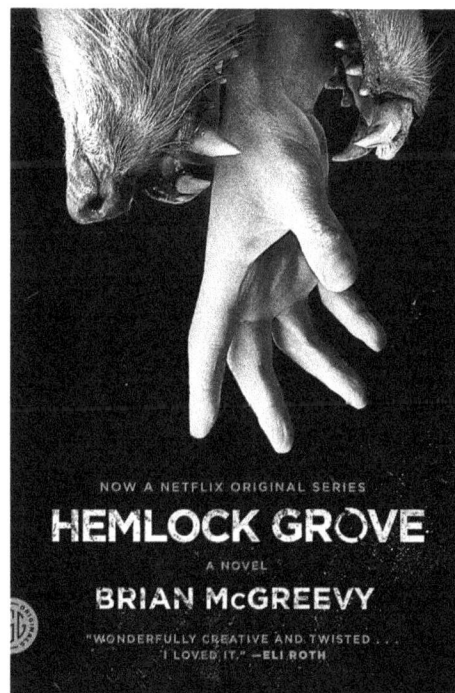

Above is another example of a striking cover that uses a type element and an image element to attract attention. The large letter "H" with vertical type gets your attention, and I think the illustration of the monster's arm is intriguing enough to make me, at least,

The cover was reworked after the book was picked up for a Netflix Original Series (above). Note they switched to photo-real images probably as a tie-in to the TV series. It's a striking cover, but I think I like the original better.

11

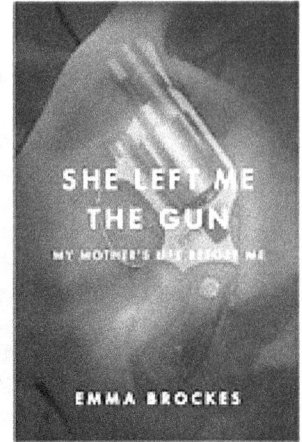

Above are some other striking examples to help you get the idea.

Take a look at your existing book's cover. Is it everything it could be? Go to Amazon and search some of the top books in the same category. Compare their covers to yours. Is your cover appropriate for its category/genre? Is it eye-catching or is it busy, fuzzy looking, illegible? Does it do its job even at thumbnail size or are you losing potential buyers because they're turned-off by your cover? If you answered no to any of these questions, it's time to rethink and redesign.

Self-published authors maintain control over nearly every aspect of the book, but that doesn't mean doing everything yourself—that can be overwhelming. If cover design makes you quake in your boots, consult an expert and *take his or her advice* so that their resulting cover does its job and doesn't end up as a bad example in an article like this!

———

Robin Surface, owner of Fideli Publishing Inc., has personally created hundreds of book covers as well as formatted the text for more than 700 books. Her company guides authors through the publishing process. Find Fideli Publishing at www.fidelipublishing.com

CHARACTER IS DESTINY

Mark Rubinstein
Author of *Mad Dog House* and *Love Gone Mad*

People often talk about a novel being plot-driven or character-driven. For me, that can be an artificial distinction. For my taste, the best novels—those that capture me and make me feel sorry the read is coming to an end—are those driven by *both* plot and by the protagonist's character or personality.

I've always felt the most engaging novels are those whose narrative drives involve conflict and uncertainty. They're novels whose plot—along with other attributes—makes me wonder *what's going to happen next.* In essence, I've always believed a good story is quite disturbing or plumbs a deep truth—one that's either obvious (think of Gillian Flynn's *Gone Girl*) or draws me on some level of which I may be unaware (think of Scott Turow's *Presumed Innocent* or Jane Hamilton's *A Map of the World*). In my view, a novel's plot is vital for it to be compelling.

For a novel to be really enjoyable, you must also care about the main character. Plot twists and conflicting situations can be engrossing, but for the novel to *really* work, the reader must feel for and identify on some level with the protagonist.

All situations about people involve three components: thinking, feeling, and behavior. A really good novel—using various devices of the craft—draws the reader into the protagonist's thoughts and feelings (emotionally and bodily). These elements often derive from the character's past and inform his or her behavior as the plot unfolds.

In a sense, the protagonist's character drives the novel's momentum. Think of Seymour Levov in Philip Roth's *American Pastoral*; Tom Wingo in Pat

Conroy's *The Prince of Tides*; Sherman McCoy in Tom Wolfe's *The Bonfire of the Vanities*; and Stingo, Nathan, or Sophie in William Styron's *Sophie's Choice*. Or, Ahab in *Moby Dick*. These wonderfully drawn characters' inner conflicts thrust the narrative flow in compelling directions. A great plotline with a poorly defined protagonist renders the novel anemic, hollow, and unsatisfying.

A compelling plot creates the potential for a great read. And, a vividly drawn character adds to the novel's power and lure. In a real way, character *is* destiny. It gives a story muscle, guts, and soul. The protagonist's character forms the tissue holding the plot together and propels it in one or another direction. Plot and character go hand-in-hand. A richly depicted *character* negotiating the rigors of a compelling *plot* provides a great read.

Mark Rubinstein was born in Brooklyn, New York. He graduated from New York University with a degree in business administration. He then served in the army and ended up as a field medic tending to paratroopers of the 82nd Airborne Division. He was so taken with these experiences that after his discharge, he re-entered NYU as a premed student. He entered medical school at the State University of New York's Downstate Medical Center. As a medical student, he developed an interest in psychiatry, discovering in that specialty the same thing he realized in reading fiction: every patient has a compelling story to tell. He became a board-certified psychiatrist practicing in New York City.

In addition to running his private practice he developed an interest in forensic psychiatry because the drama and conflict of the cases and courtrooms tapped into his personality style. He also taught psychiatric residents, interns, psychologists, and social workers at New York Presbyterian Hospital and became a clinical assistant professor at Cornell University's medical school.

Before turning to fiction, Rubinstein coauthored five medical self-help books: *The First Encounter: The Beginnings in Psychotherapy*, *The Complete Book of Cosmetic Facial Surgery*, *New Choices: the Latest Options in Treating Breast Cancer*, *Heartplan: A Complete Program for Total Fitness of Heart & Mind*, and *The Growing Years: A Guide to Your Child's Emotional Development from Birth to Adolescence*.

Rubinstein lives in Connecticut with his wife and as many dogs as she will allow in the house. He still practices psychiatry and is busily writing more novels. *Mad Dog House*, his first novel, was named a Finalist for the 2012 ForeWord Reviews Book of the Year Award (Thriller & Suspense). His second novel, *Love Gone Mad*, coming out this September, is available for preorder through Mark's website, www.MarkRubinstein-Author.com

INTERNATIONAL LOCALES: WHY AND HOW TO USE THEM IN YOUR NOVEL

Allan Topol, author *The Russian Endgame*

When I wrote my first novel, *The Fourth of July War*, the agent I was working with said, "It's good you use foreign settings. Readers like them."

I didn't think much about it at the time because I was writing a novel of international intrigue. Of course, there were foreign locales in addition to Washington.

Now my ninth novel, *The Russian Endgame*, was published in September. That book, like all the others, has numerous foreign locales. The action moves among Moscow, Beijing, Paris, Bali, Corsica, and Prague. The foreign locales are critical to this novel, which deals with a resurgent Russia and its alliance with China to assassinate an American president and steal cutting edge U.S. defense technology.

Over the years, as I've spoken with readers, the words of that agent have resonated. Readers do like foreign locales. If the action occurs in a place they've visited, they will relive their trip and enjoy recognizing places the author mentions. If they haven't been there, they will travel vicariously with the author to the foreign locale and hopefully enjoy the trip as well as the novel.

So my advice is that if you have a choice of setting a scene in Paris or Pittsburgh, opt for Paris. Barcelona or Bridgeport, select Barcelona. Your readers will appreciate it.

Then the question becomes which foreign places to select and how to deal with them in your novel. Often the story dictates the place. For my seventh novel, *The China Gambit*, which concerns the growth of military power in China, some scenes had to take place in Beijing.

Other times, the author will have a choice. In *The Russian Endgame*, it was important that a critical scene near the end of the novel take place outside of the United States. I selected Prague but could have easily chosen other cities in central Europe. However, I had been to Prague. I understood the characteristics of the surrounding area. Those were perfect for the action that unfolds.

When I had visited Prague, it was purely for pleasure. I had no intention of putting a scene in a book there. Other places I have gone to specifically for book research.

This brings me to a critical point. If at all possible, use places that you know from at least one visit. In order to make the scene come alive for the reader, you must not only visualize, but also feel the place yourself. If you want to use a place that you haven't visited, try to go there before you write your novel or certainly before you finish it. Take careful notes of what you see, and photographs. Most important, talk to people there to understand the place. When you get home, check material on the Internet and in books to confirm your impressions.

Sometimes, it won't be possible to visit a place that's critical for a novel. In my novel, *Enemy of My Enemy*, which involved Russia, Syria, Israel, and the United States as well as Syria's effort to obtain nuclear weapons from Russia, the final scene takes place in Baku, Azerbaijan, which was critical because of its geography. I had planned to fly to Baku where I'd never been and even had plane and hotel reservations. At that moment, it appeared as if the first Gulf War would erupt (which it did).

My travel agent warned that I would be likely to get to Baku but she didn't know how I'd get out because she expected all air traffic to the region to be suspended. I decided to cancel the trip, but because of a publishing deadline I had to get enough background to write the scene. I turned to books and the Internet. Living in Washington I was able to get materials from the Azerbaijan Embassy. I hope that I described the city accurately. No one has told me I didn't, and readers have no hesitation in doing so.

In using international locales, the author must deal with certain practical issues. Language is one. Do you tell the reader which characters are speaking English and which a foreign language? Unless there is some specific reason for doing so, I tend to ignore the language issue and write the novel as if anyone is speaking English.

There is the question of maps: to include them in the beginning of the book or not. Authors are divided. Personally, I reject them because I would prefer to have readers following the action rather than stopping to turn back to look at a map.

The author also has to worry about political changes in the foreign country if those are relevant to his novel. I used the Shah of Iran in *The Fourth of July War*. Happily, he wasn't deposed until after the novel was published. Unhappily, the change of government in Iran killed my movie option.

Accuracy about geography and other details is critical. An author must get the facts right about locales — domestic or international. I once read in a novel from a bestselling author that a character in Paris asked the cab driver to drop him off in front of the American Embassy on Boulevard Franklin Roosevelt. Since the American Embassy is not on Boulevard Franklin Roosevelt, that made the author's entire book suspect in my mind.

This anecdote sums up the discussion of international locales. Yes, the author gains a great deal in using them, but there is a price to pay: travel time and expense making sure you get it right.

Those are offset by other advantages. For example, you may have a wonderful dinner in a bistro on the left bank in Paris with an outstanding bottle of wine all in the name of research. You may also pretend to be living your hero's life, if only for an evening.

———

Allan Topol is the national bestselling author of eight novels of international intrigue, including *Spy Dance*. He is a graduate of Carnegie Institute of Technology, who majored in chemistry, abandoned science, and obtained a law degree from Yale University. He has traveled extensively, researching dramatic locations for his novels. You can join him on Facebook and sign up for his newsletter. Allan is available for speaking opportunities on subjects of international affairs, dealt with in his novels. Visit his website: www.allantopol.com

BOOKS ON WRITING

Here are some helpful books you might want to read to help you with your writing:

WRITING CRAFT

On Writing Well: The Classic Guide to Writing Nonfiction. by William Zinsser

Walking on Water: Reflections on Faith and Art by Madeleine L'Engle

Finding Your Writer's Voice: A Guide to Creative Fiction. by Frank & Wall

Crafting The Personal Essay: A Guide for Writing and Publishing Creative Non-Fiction. by Dinty Moore

FOUNDATION

The Anatomy of Story: 22 Steps to Becoming a Master Storyteller by John Truby

The Making of a Story: A Norton Guide to Writing Fiction and Nonfiction by Alice LaPlante

Story: Substance, Structure, Style and the Principles of Screenwriting by Robert McKee

The Way of Story: The Craft & Soul of Writing by Catherine Ann Jones

The Writers Journey: Mythic Structure for Writers, 3rd Edition by Christopher Vogler

Stealing Fire from the Gods: The Complete Guide to Story for Writers and Filmmakers (2nd Edition) by James Bonnet

How to Kill a Dragon: Aspects of Indo-European Poetics by Calvert Watkins

The Hero's Journey: Joseph Campbell on His Life and Work (The Collected Works of Joseph Campbell) by Joseph Campbell

CHARACTER

The Complete Writer's Guide to Heroes and Heroines by Tami Cowden

Characters, Emotion & Viewpoint: Techniques and Exercises for Crafting Dynamic Characters and Effective Viewpoints (Write Great Fiction) by Nancy Kress

Elements of Fiction Writing—Characters & Viewpoint by Orson Scott Card

INSPIRATION

On Writing: A Memoir of the .Craft by Stephen King (*Also memoir and one of the best books I've read about the art of writing.*)

Page after Page. by Heather Sellers

The War of Art: Break Through the Blocks and Win Your Inner Creative Battles. by Steven Pressfield

MEMOIRS

Writing Down the Bones: Freeing the Writer Within . by Natalie Goldberg

Bird by Bird: Some Instructions on Writing and Life . by Anne Lamott

EDITING & STYLE

The Elements of Style (4th Edition). by William Strunk and E. B. White

The Curious Case of the Misplaced Modifier: How to Solve the Mysteries of Weak Writing. by Bonnie Trenga

The AP Styleboook (for reference)

Fine-Tuning by Roy Peter Clark

100 Ways to Improve Your Writing (Mentor Series) by Gary Provost

Stein On Writing: A Master Editor of Some of the Most Successful Writers of Our Century Shares His Craft Techniques and Strategies by Sol Stein

CRAZY BUSINESS OF TV WRITING

Stanley Dyrector, playwright and author

You'll have to excuse me for skirting names of certain people who may be dead or alive, but I feel more comfortable that way at the moment.

Winter, 1981:

Nowadays I'm on the straight and narrow. I'm driving a limousine for the Kosmos Livery Service. Whoopie! (Thank the Gods of Olympus!) I needed a job so bad, you wouldn't believe. I'm giving you the low-down on how things were before, as I now sit in a limo in the driveway waiting for a client, to drive as directed (AD) when they exit the ritzy hotel lobby.

Let us flash back, like movie magic, about six months.

Mr. Casce, our oafish, sharp as a tack landlord, has us prisoner in our two-bedroom apartment (almost literally). He's outside our door this evening because we owe him rent and have run out of excuses to give him. I'm only a week late this time, but I know he won't cut us slack anymore. Casce's presence gives my wife Tess and I palpitations of the heart. The word heart is like a foreign country to him, similar to the reputations of lawyers.

You heard the story of these lawyers going scuba diving and a whole school of hungry sharks spot 'em and turn away, leaving them alone. It's called professional courtesy. To be up front, I'm tired of hiding from Casce. I'm not a crook…have just had a run of bad luck lately; no TV script sales. We've been great

tenants for years—he even came to our wedding in our apartment. He's looking to get us out so he can get higher rent.

Here's the kind of landlord Casce is. There was a time we had a leaky toilet, which was running day and night driving me bonkers for two months, to where I had a helluva time trying to sleep nights. He ignored our constant requests to have it fixed. But then one early morning, out of the blue, by surprise, he just lets himself into our apartment with his master key, without warning or any notice. Chrissakes! My wife Tess is suddenly frightened…she's wearing a short slip, and I'm almost naked as a jaybird, with torn skivvies that I'm holding up so they don't fall down off my tush. Tess is nudging me, thinking we're being burglarized. I react stupidly by giving her a shove back into the bedroom and closing the door….

Whoa, people! Hold on a second…change of plan. The doorman of this ritzy hotel just told me he wants me to move my limo, bring it around Sunset Boulevard, and come back to the same spot I'm in… he'll keep an eye out for my clients. Doorman is king.

Back again. Client isn't here yet. That's the limousine business—wait, wait, wait.

Getting back to landlord Casce, you'd think if he showed up like that he'd have had a plumber at hand, like any sane, good landlord would. But no, he's cheap and he wants to save a few bucks. I'm watching him fix the toilet; he fixes things with chewing gum…half-assed, the results a disaster. He flushes once, the toilet overflows, flooding the floor all over, soaking my socks and the living room carpet. We had to go to friends' to clean up for the next few days. You've heard of the song "Send in the Clowns"?' I changed it to "Send in the Goddamn Plumbers You Cheap Bastard."

Now back on that; later that evening, inside our place we're listening to Casce's wheezes while he stands outside our front door. Unbeknownst to him I saw him park in back of our two-story, four-unit apartment building earlier and alerted Tess, but it was too late to escape. We're hoping he'll give up his snooping nonsense and call it a night. My silent mantra is "Casce, just blow away." Shakespeare's words are, "Dream on MacDuff." If I told the shmuck the truth, that I'm expecting a check from my kid brother who lives in New York, he'd tell me "Tough cocky, I need my rent."

He's messing with the door lock now and stops a minute. "Mischief, thou art afoot." I'm thinking. What's up his sleeve? Of course, same scenario…he's listening to see if we're really at home. We're quieter than church mice. I heard his astrological sign was Leo. Leo's are arrogant and pugnacious piss ants, particularly when they're short. He rips off a fart that you could hear in Buffalo…yup. 3,000 miles away. He's got a Napoleanic complex, and lives under the illusion he's God's gift to unattached females stuck on their rent payments.

Ooops! The door lock's turning. Satan is trying to enter. I'm chewing garlic—there're folk stories that say it keeps devils away. I'm a believer. I manage to keep up my own false macho façade by gesturing with a raised fist at the door, reassuring Tess I'm like a Mike Tyson. But I am really the magician, no need of a fighter. Everything suddenly ceases. Casce has discovered he's screwed; his master key cannot complete its job. Earlier in the day Falstaff took from his penny jar, cashed them in, and I added a dead bolt to the door. The last thing we heard that night was angry rants and banging with clenched fists on our door, Casce shouting loud anathemas.

In Brooklyn, as a kid growing up, I'd be in the candy store reading the comic books and Casce's rants would've been depicted with a cloud above his character's numb-nuts head muttering, "Curses, foiled again!"

So now, readers, you have some idea about how things were for me before I got this limo gig: In hock up the wazoo. It got to such a point of desperation I was within an inch of jumping onto the Hollywood Freeway nearby with a rag in my hand giving quickie window washes, figuring if I lived doing it, I'd go into partnership with Windex.

I was making a helluva living as a scribe/actor, fat city, for a long time. But bad things happen to good people like that book says. Earnings as a TV writer were drier than Death Valley. I don't count as income my deluge of wealth from show business: the twelve buck residual check I got from 20th Century Fox for a movie I acted in years ago called, "Snipers Ridge," or a Writers Guild royalty check for eighteen cents from Budapest/ Romania, for the reruns of a Wagon Train I wrote with my deceased collaborator.

My wife, Tess, bless her heart, slipped and fell on a crack on our street, and got her a bum back. She can't go do cocktail waitressing in between writing jobs anymore. Tess is a clever, funny, comedic writer, who wastes her afternoons hung up watching those stupid ABC soaps—"All My Children," "Ryan's Hope," and other stuff that's strictly crappola.

I got the limo gig at Kosmos because of my friend Peter Grillo, who was driving for them. We was having a beer at a local hang out for writers, actors, and singles called the Raincheck Room, on Santa Monica Boulevard, the kind of place where a gal doesn't have to look over her shoulder to be hit on by some jerk. Peter understood my distress, and like a true pal recommended me to his bosses. I had driving experience. I also used to drive taxis. You've got to understand about being a writer in La-La-Land…out here, grief and heartache go together, like the Hollywood Jungle of Sodom and Gomorrah.

My client, whom I'll call Ms. Hoity Toity, is tall and trim, fiftyish with short dark hair, wears tortoise shell glasses, has a Prada bag strapped around her shoulder, like she's carrying a rod or precious jewels, close to the vest, know what I mean; she also wears a serious sourpuss. I'm aware of nuances and subtleties in our daily lives because I'm a professional screenwriter. I wrote episodes of the TV series "Kojak" and other cop shows.

I glance in the rearview. When she got in my client, Ms. Hoity, never gave me a destination where we were going. And I had to get away from the front door of the hotel because it was getting jammed up. Ms. Hoity has her attention riveted on her tiny black address book lying in her lap, and, every so often, she strikes down fiercely on it with her pencil stub, precisely, in a premeditated warplane bombing attack dive on an enemy target. She takes a puff off her long cigarette, blows smoke out of her mouth like Bette Davis did in the movies, and grins, pleased. My guess is she's either a serial killer or something a little less innocuous. Now if she was planning her killings along our driving route, and gets caught, paranoid me thinks I'll be one of the usual suspects, and held as an accomplice. But then again, maybe she's just planning her stops for business—but what kind? Where? I asked her when she got in, "Where to, ma'am?" She was silent, like, no response. I ask her again now. She's lost somewhere in thought. I'm feeling like a pesky moth attracted to the burning orange tip at the end of her cigarette. I again ask her, "Where are we going, ma'am?" It's a rule of thumb in the limo biz—clients are immune from most anything. I've had clients throw paper cups at me and try to get me high with sticking cocaine up my nostrils.

Take nothing for granted was the rule when I attended the company's chauffeur driving school across the street in the park from the major hotel we serviced. In school, chauffeurs were taught how the company worked, and Cy, the old timer who was teaching, would drill us numerous times a day that we were the company's face. Cy was given his position by the gay gentleman who owned the company. We learned the rates: limos were at $50 an hour, with an automatic 15% gratuity for ourselves. Cy relished tutoring us on the extra cash tips we could make if we followed his disciplined rules: Always be polite and courteous, and have your car well stocked with the alcohol the company supplied—which you had to account for. After Cy's prolonged talks on theory of the operation of your motor vehicle, he'd take us in a limo where he had each one of us drive while he sat in the front seat passenger side and excitedly gave us orders on how to handle the limousine. He was the college professor, telling us how much gas to give on the pedal when we went around the snake-like curves on Sunset Boulevard going east. His commands would use terms such as pennies, to slow down, dimes to be slower, and quarters to step on it. Yes, it was quite a meaningful education, in which I did receive a diploma for excellence.

Ms. Hoity's got the look of money—hooray for the rich! Hooray! I'm going to call my fair lady client, out of respect, Ms. New York. *Brrr!* She brought the chilly climate. She is stuck up. (Or am I too sensitive?) She's said less than a handful of words since we've started our journey. I did give her a cheerful, "Howdy, ma'am," when the doorman at the Beverly Hills Hotel escorted her and opened the door for her to slip in the back. She handed him an ace as she got in.

First thing, she helped herself to mints I stock for clients in the side tray, and she chewed on 'em while puffing away on a cigarette, making like a chimney. More than annoying. I gave up tobacco. I turn on the AC full blast, clearing the air. Ah, yes, it's great to breathe! She's all hung up with the addresses. Then she mutters, "Where's the phone?" I tell her it's out of order, but on the rear window shelf. She frowns. "Is it really?" she asks. I nod yes, it really was out. She mutters an, "Oh, shit."

Here's a flashback: I remember my first week on the job, chauffeuring Ed Bradley of "60 minutes." I picked him up from another hotel where my company didn't keep its cars. But before I leave our garage to pick him up, the dispatcher says the company's worried that CBS might not pay for Ed Bradley's phone use. And the Hilton Hotel, which called our company, may try to dispute charges on phone bills. My mouth drops, I can't believe what I'm hearing. I was going to say, "Are you crazy? This is Ed Bradley, '60 Minutes'! Schmucks!" But quickly I shut up. Like the absurdity of it. "60 Minutes" is going to stiff my company?

So, when I got there to pick Ed Bradley up and we're driving, he asks, "Where's the phone?" I lied. Said it was out of order. Gee did that hurt. It really, honest and truly pissed me off.

Stanley Dyrector was born in Brooklyn, New York. Beginning his career as an actor, he switched to writing, where he found much success. His TV writing credits include such popular shows as Wagon Train and Slattery's People. He and his wife, Joyce, teamed up and wrote for daytime TV soaps on ABC, as well as hour radio dramas and comedies for Sears Radio Theatre and Mutual Radio Theatre. Dyrector's 2-act Vietnam-era play, *A Pelican of the Wilderness,* was deemed by *LA Times* critic John Mahoney as "Outstanding." His award-winning interview show, "The Stanley Dyrector Show," can be seen in various locales and on the Internet. Find him on Facebook.

TAXI REST

Stanley Dyrector, playwright and author

In Hollywood being an actor is a precarious trade. I've been one for a long time—decades. We actors in Tinseltown have to develop survival skills. If you are not God's gift to the world, or have a steady acting job in a television series that keeps you gainfully employed, or are not a millionaire, you may find yourself just crap out of luck! (I like euphemisms.) And if you are legit, pockets empty without a soul. Tcha. That's life, isn't it? It's rough and tumble in any man's language.

My father, Ruby, taught me how to drive when I was a teenager. I learned in a Willy's Jeep at the gas station he managed in Canarsie. Eventually I drove the old Willy's Jeep all alone in back of the station's huge vacant weeded lot, where further south was a swamp land where an old rusted Chevy body lay, its engine stolen, an irony in its own automobile graveyard, but yet a home to field rats and skunk.

If you knew how to drive and were lucky enough to own a car, back in my day, you were hot stuff! It was freedom. You'd get to pick up girls and go for joyrides. It was extremely important for me to learn to drive. Independence. So, whenever my father's boss was not around, Pop'd be in the Jeep with me, in the passenger seat giving me a litany of instructions on what to do and not to do. The Jeep was a floor stick shift. Riding with me, Pop must've felt like he was on a bucking bronco in a rodeo. He was a participant of bumpy rides, starts and sudden jerking forward, and holding on so as not to bang his head into the windshield.

Alone, I'd throw the clutch driven car into every one of its five gearshifts and speed, and pretend I was an Indianapolis 500 driver, sometime yelling, "Woo! Woo!" I cringe now reliving the times I took sharp turns a bit too sharp for my own good and almost rolled over. Pshew! Coulda got hurt, or curtains. Yikes. Thanks to the Gods I survived my follies.

Not to change the subject, but one of the perks of helping out at the gas station, a highlight, was meeting Miss Rheingold (a popular beer), who was a frequent customer there and undoubtedly charmed by Pop's personality. Mary had green eyes, greener than I'd ever seen before…green as I'd imagined Ireland was with its shamrocks. Yes, they were as green as the sea below the ship I would be stationed on as a sailor in my future. (By the way, back then, a gas station was also called a service station, because you'd service the car by wiping its windows and checking the oil, water, and battery fluid, besides pumping Ethyl).

Driving a taxi was a good fit for me because of my pop's tutelage. Then, I was in my twenties, in Hollywood, and needed the important bread and butter jobs to get by. I held many others over the years, including private chauffeur, limousine driver, tour bus driver, TV writer, radio writer, VIP head usher for "The Steve Allen Show" on Vine Street in Hollywood, etcetera. Folks, if you ever have a chance to see a

"Nightline" ABC rerun of when Frank Sinatra died, you will see and hear me talk about the Chairman of the Board in one of the vignettes as I drove past his house in Beverly Hills in 1990s. Can you imagine? I am in the company of many celebrities who were filmed for that TV presentation, among them Robert DeNiro.

Eventually dear reader, I'd like to tell you about one particular experience I had while in the taxi business, which sticks out in my memory. It happened sometime in the 1960s…. (By the way, there were many more incidents and stories)

The taxicab company I drove for had a telephone callbox on the Sunset Strip, close to "The Interlude" and the "Crescendo" nightclubs, which were almost next door to each other, like book ends. Both clubs shared the same sidewalk and were maybe about fifteen or twenty feet apart. At the Interlude, when you entered you'd prepare to climb a flight of stairs, which took you directly into the intimate club, where there was a prominent piano on display for performers. The "Crescendo," on the other hand, was much bigger, had a much bigger cover charge, was more lavish, definitely high-end, and was obviously the antithesis of the laissez faire Interlude. Crescendo catered to well-heeled big spenders, men in three-piece Pierre Cardin suits and ladies in Oleg Cassini's latest fashion. Stars, the stature of singers like Ella Fitzgerald, Peggy Lee, and comedian Lennie Bruce, performed there regularly. Crescendo's performers' list must've read like an old MGM publicity ad…"more stars than there are in heaven." Joey Lewis, a popular big star comedian who drank like a fish and performed his act there, appeared drunk as a skunk and talked about the ponies, women, and gambling. His life was characterized by Frank Sinatra in the successful film *The Joker is Wild*, in which Frank sang the song "All the Way."

The Interlude nightclub would have a mixed bag of talent, where you could see performers like Frances Faye play piano and sing—sing some of her songs with the raunchiest lyrics. She was an endearing light on the Strip, someone way ahead of the curve. She was a self-outed lesbian, when gay people were extremely oppressed in West Hollywood. One ditty Frances sang began like this: "I'm Francis Faye and I'm gay-gay-gay!"

Now that I think we are up to speed and on the same page I will tell you what happened this one night outside the Interlude. I went to our taxi phone and could not help but see this guy with glasses, who was slight of built, standing outside the door of the Interlude, gazing unhappily out onto the surrounding streets and sidewalks, undoubtedly checking the busy thoroughfare out, with cars whizzing by, uncaring of the person on the sidewalk. So, after I was through with the taxi phone, out of curiosity I engaged him in a conversation. It lasted for a number of minutes. He had a New York accent, like I did, and this was one of the first times he was performing in Los Angeles. He was disappointed in the fact that there was nobody upstairs to see him perform. He was a comedian. His name was Woody Allen.

Stanley Dyrector's award-winning interview show, "The Stanley Dyrector Show," can be seen in various locales and on the Internet. Find him on Facebook.

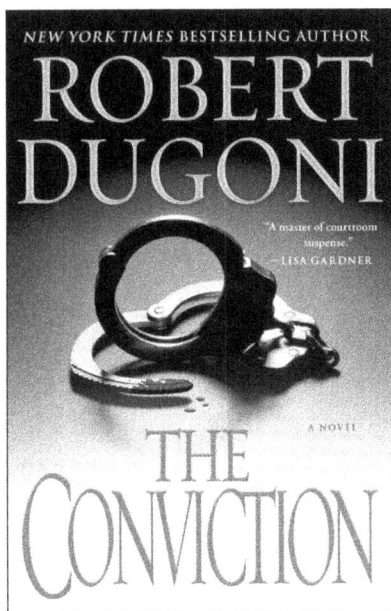

THE CONVICTION

Author: Robert Dugoni
Page count: 384
ISBN: 978-1451606720
Formats: Hardcover Paperback, ebook, audio
Find the author:
www.robertdugoni.com

In this gripping, high-octane thriller by critically acclaimed *New York Times* bestselling author Robert Dugoni, a father takes the law into his own hands to save his son, who is trapped in a juvenile detention center from hell.

Lawyer David Sloane is desperate to get through to his troubled teenage son Jake. Still reeling from the devastating loss of his mother in a brutal murder, Jake has spiraled out of control and Sloane has barely been able to keep him out of jail. So when his old friend, detective Tom Molia, suggests that they take their sons on a guys-only camping trip, Sloane gratefully accepts.

What Sloane imagines will be the perfect excursion turns into a horrifying nightmare when the boys are arrested for vandalizing a general store late at night while their fathers are asleep. The next morning, before Sloane and Molia even realize they're gone, their sons are tried, convicted, and sentenced by the presiding judge to six months in the county wilderness detention camp, Fresh Start. For the teenagers, a grueling physical and psychological ordeal begins.

As Sloane fights the conviction against the boys, he discovers that local judge Earl Boykin's authority seems to extend far beyond the confines of his courtroom. Meanwhile, on the inside, Jake is forced to grow up quickly and soon learns the hard way that this detention center has a very different purpose than rehabilitating troubled youths.

With their legal options exhausted, Sloane and Molia will do anything to save their sons—even mount a daring rescue operation that could win the boys their freedom...or cost all of them their lives.

Reviews:

Chosen one of five Cool Summer Reads for Hot Summer Nights

— *Tucson Citizen*

One of the best legal thriller writers in the business unleashes another stellar effort with "The Conviction." ...The names John Grisham and Scott Turow are mentioned when discussing the legal thriller genre. Robert Dugoni is as good, if not better.

—*The Associated Press*

Unexpected twists...shocking surprises no one could've predicted.

—*Chicago Book Examiner*

[A]n exhilarating story that is crisply written and full of unexpected plot twists.

—*Tucson Citizen*

Dugoni's latest serves up the perfect mix of action, emotion and courtroom drama, so much so that "The Conviction" isn't just the best legal thriller of the year, it's one of the best thrillers period.

—*Providence Journal*

Dugoni knows the legal world well and produces a complicated puzzle that will resonate with fans of Grisham, and provide a jolt of adrenaline.

—*Los Angeles Review of Books*

Dugoni is at his best in the action scenes, which are the foundation of his narrative. Fans of John Grisham and Scott Turow will be pleased with this offering.

—*Library Journal, May 2012*

Peopled with the usual contingent of sadists and victims, the plot's fuse starts burning. Lawyer Sloane, Detective Molia and a posse of trusty associates skilled in the latest morally dubious investigative methods uncover a startling conspiracy. Unlike revenge, justice seems to be a dish best served warm, and pursuit is hot.

—*Kirkus, May 2012*

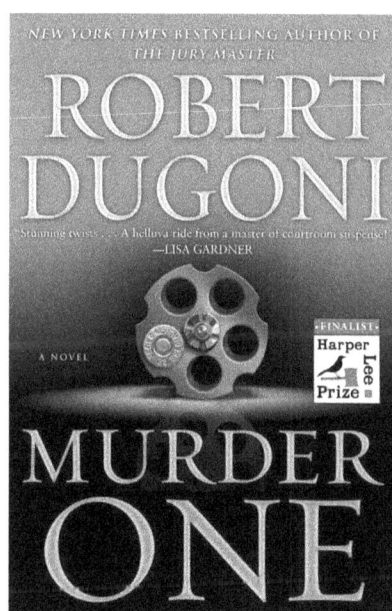

MURDER ONE

Author: Robert Dugoni
Page count: 386
ISBN10: 1451606699
Formats: Hardcover, Paperback, ebook, audio
Find the author: www.robertdugoni.com

Finalist for The Harper Lee Award for Excellence in Legal Fiction Writing and winner of the popular vote

New York Times bestselling author Robert Dugoni delivers another gripping legal thriller in his popular David Sloane series. The case? Defending the woman he loves against a charge of murder.

A year after the devastating murder of his wife, attorney David Sloane has returned to Seattle after three months in Mexico. At a black-tie dinner where he's been persuaded to give the keynote address, Sloane reconnects with Barclay Reid, opposing counsel in his most prominent case. Barclay is suffering from her own personal tragedy—the death of her teenage daughter from a drug overdose. In the aftermath, Barclay has begun an intense crusade against the Russian drug traffickers she holds responsible for her daughter's death, pursuing them with a righteousness that matches Sloane's own zeal for justice. Despite their adversarial past, Sloane is drawn to Barclay, and for the first time since his wife died, he finds himself beginning to have romantic feelings again.

But when Barclay's crusade stalls and a Russian drug dealer turns up dead, she stands accused of murder, and Sloane is her chosen defender. Amid the swirling media frenzy, in his first criminal case, Sloane finds himself once again in harm's way, while mounting evidence suggests that Barclay is a woman with many secrets—and may not be quite as innocent as she seems.

With his signature fast-paced, page-turning action and exhilarating plot twists, Robert Dugoni once again proves why he's so often been named the heir to Grisham's literary throne.

Top Five Thriller of the Year
—*Los Angeles Review of Books*

Top Five Thriller of the Year
— *Library Journal*

Top Thriller of the Year
— *New York Public Library*

Top Ten Thriller of the Year
— *Miami Examiner*

Reviews:

Dugoni knows the legal world well and produces a complicated puzzle that will resonate with fans of Grisham, and provide a jolt of adrenaline.
—*Los Angeles Times Review of Books*

Dugoni should be cloned. His expertise, knowledge, and excellent writing makes for books that are surefire page-turners.
—*Miami Examiner*

Tight plotting and well-developed characters push Dugoni to the head of the legal thriller pack in what is probably his finest book to date. John Grisham and Scott Turow fans should add Dugoni to their list of must-reads.
—*Library Journal*, Starred Review

Dugoni has often been described as a challenger to Turow and the other big names in the legal-thriller genre, but at this point, he's claimed his own position on the A-list. A must read for fans of courtroom drama, from Grisham to Turow to Erle Stanley Gardner.
—*Booklist*

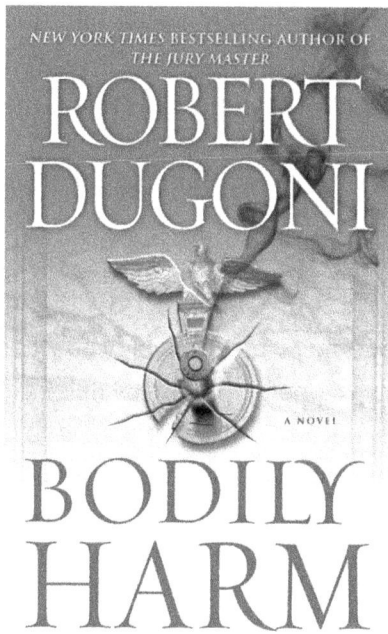

BODILY HARM

Author: Robert Dugoni
Page count: 480
ISBN10: 1416592989
Formats: Hardcover, Paperback, ebook, audio
Find the author: www. robertdugoni.com

New York Times bestselling author Robert Dugoni returns with his most exhilarating thriller to date, a pulse-pounding story of corporate greed, espionage, and the lengths one man is willing to go for justice.

Bodily Harm opens with a big win for David Sloane and his new partner, Tom Pendergrass, in a malpractice case centered on the death of a young child. But on the heels of this seeming victory, an unlikely character—toy designer Kyle Horgan—comes forward to tell Sloane that he's gotten it all wrong: Horgan's the one who's truly responsible for the little boy's death and possibly others, not the pediatrician Sloane has just proven guilty.

Ordinarily, Sloane might have dismissed such a person as a crackpot, but something about this case has always troubled him—something that he couldn't quite pinpoint. When Sloane tries to follow up with Horgan, he finds the man's apartment a shambles—ransacked by unknown perpetrators. Horgan has vanished without a trace. Together with his longtime investigative partner Charles Jenkins, Sloane reexamines his clients' son's death and digs deeper into Horgan's claims, forcing him to enter the billion-dollar, cutthroat toy industry. As Sloane gets closer to the truth, he trips a wire that leads to a shocking chain of events that nearly destroys him.

To get to the bottom of it all and find justice for the families harmed, Sloane must keep in check his overwhelming desire for revenge. Full of nail-bitingly tense action scenes as well as edge-of-your-seat courtroom drama, *Bodily Harm* finds Robert Dugoni at the very top of his game.

Reviews:

One of the Top Five Thrillers of the Year

—*Library Journal*

Dugoni has been knocking on the legal-thriller door for a while, and his latest firmly establishes him in the top echelon of the genre. Tense and shocking from the beginning to the surprising end, this is Dugoni s best book yet. Prior knowledge of his other David Sloane novels is not necessary, but they will be eagerly sought out by new readers who finish this one.

—*Booklist – Starred Review*

Robert Dugoni does so many things well in his terrific *Bodily Harm* that it's hard to know where to start. Blending the best of Scott Turow and John Grisham with a hefty measure of the cutting-edge Michael Crichton thrillers *Disclosure* and *Airframe*, Dugoni's latest is a smooth, cross-genre hybrid that works on every level. In that respect, *Bodily Harm* most resembles Word of Honor, still Nelson DeMille's masterwork. No Turow or Grisham tale ever had this kind of depth, color and breathless plotting, and the result brands Dugoni as the undisputed king of the legal thriller.

—*Providence Journal*

An intriguing premise incorporated with lots of action makes this a real page-turner, but the courtroom is where the heart of this story lies. The combination of legal, corporate, and even some political thrills will appeal to fans of Richard North Patterson and Joseph Finder.

—*Library Journal*

Dugoni has developed a briskly paced tale that incorporates headlines and heartbreak. Go ahead and pack it in your beach tote — and don't forget the sunscreen!

—*The Bellingham Herald*

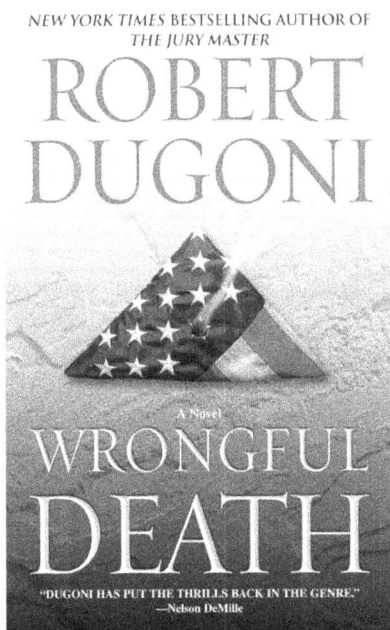

WRONGFUL DEATH

Author: Robert Dugonni
Page count: 480
ISBN: 978-1410416810
Formats: Hardcover, Paperback, ebook, audio
Find the author:
www.robertdugoni.com

Just minutes after winning a $1.6 million wrongful-death verdict, attorney David Sloane confronts the one case that threatens to blemish his unbeaten record in the courtroom. Beverly Ford wants Sloane to sue the United States government and military in the mysterious death of her husband, James, a national guardsman killed in Iraq. While a decades-old military doctrine might make Ford's case impossible to win, Sloane, a former soldier himself, is compelled to find justice for the widow and her four children in what is certain to become the biggest challenge of his career.

With little hard evidence to go on, Sloane calls on his friend, reclusive former CIA agent turned private investigator Charles Jenkins, to track down the other men serving with Ford the night he died. Alarmingly, two of the four who returned home alive didn't stay that way for long, and though the mission's wheelchair bound commander now works for a civilian contractor he refuses to talk. The final—and youngest—soldier is also the most elusive, but he's their only shot at discovering the truth… if Sloane and Jenkins can keep him alive long enough to tell it.

Meanwhile, Sloane isn't the only one on a manhunt. As he propels his case into a federal courtroom, those seeking to hide the truth threaten Sloane's family, forcing his new wife Tina and stepson Jake into hiding, where they become the targets of a relentless killer. Now Sloane must race to uncover what really happened on that fatal mission, not only to bring justice to a family wronged but to keep himself and the people closest to him from becoming the next casualties...

Reviews:

Page-turning action.
—*Publishers Weekly*

An entertaining thriller. Good guys to like, villains to hiss, windmills to attack.
—*Kirkus*

Mixing the suspense of a Grisham legal thriller with the political angle of a Baldacci. Dugoni is knocking on the A-list thriller door and should be expected to enter sooner rather than later.
—*Booklist*

Robert Dugoni explodes from the tired pack of Grisham Wannabes.
—*The Seattle Times*

Robert Dugoni belongs right up there with Grisham, Martini, Levine, and the best legal novelists of our time … He is a master storyteller and keeping his characters alive becomes a challenge that unleashes a wild ride and an incredible story.

—*Mystery News*

An exciting, moving tale of loyalty, deceit, friendship, duty, greed and valor. *Wrongful Death* is an exceptional novel that not only ranks among the best of its genre, it is among the best books to be published this year.

—*Mysterious Reviews*

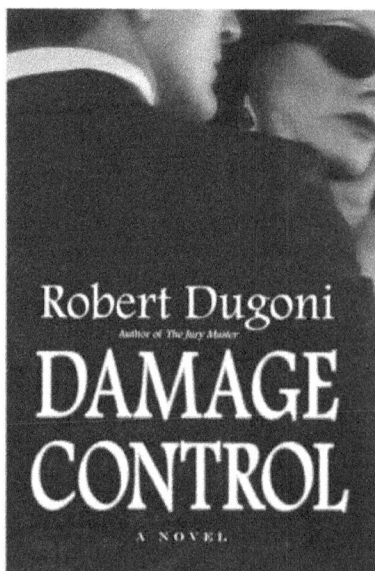

DAMAGE CONTROL

Author: Robert Dugoni
Page count: 406
ISBN: 978-0446578707
Formats: Hardcover, Paperback, ebook, audio
Find the author:
www.robertdugoni.com

#8 National Independent Booksellers List

Attorney Dana Hill is used to managing a stressful life: she's one of the most successful lawyers at Strong & Thurmond, mother to a young daughter, wife to a busy, self-involved man. But when she is diagnosed with breast cancer, and her twin brother turns up beaten to death in an apparent robbery-gone-wrong in the same week, the careful balance of Dana's life is sent into flux. Agreeing with the police that this is more than just a simple botched burglary, she begins to sift through the pieces of her brother's life, a life she thought she knew as well as her own, to find out who would want him dead and why.

But bad things happen in threes, her mother has told her. When Dana discovers her husband cheating, she throws herself headlong into the investigation. Delaying cancer treatment, she teams with an intuitive detective to find the link between a one-of-a-kind earring found in her brother's bedroom and a mysterious girlfriend no one seems to be able to identify. But those connected to the murder are beginning to turn up dead, the evidence trail is growing cold, and someone is masquerading as a police officer, cleaning up the details as they go along.

Reviews:

A page turner...fast-moving plot...A few twists will surprise even seasoned thriller readers.

—Publisher's Weekly

Dana Hill and the supporting cast are fascinating characters and they propel the narrative to its shocking conclusion. Comparisons to the early works of John Grisham and the thrillers of David Baldacci are easily warranted. Dugoni's latest is destined to damage the bestseller lists.

—Library Journal

...the plot twists keep the pages turning.

—Kirkus

The story takes off in the first chapter, and the pacing remains very fast throughout the story. This is one of those great page-turners that make time fly.

—Booklist

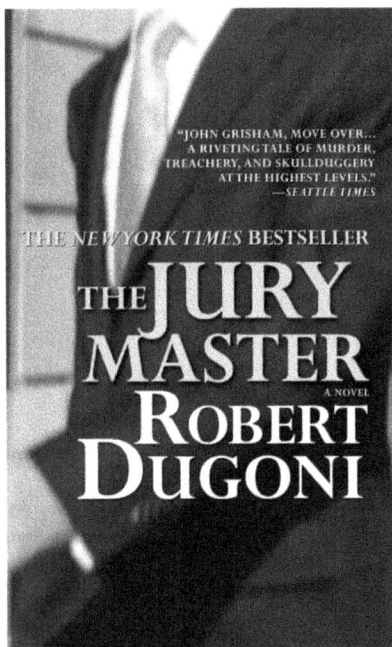

"JOHN GRISHAM, MOVE OVER...
A RIVETING TALE OF MURDER,
TREACHERY, AND SKULLDUGGERY
AT THE HIGHEST LEVELS."
—SEATTLE TIMES

THE *NEW YORK TIMES* BESTSELLER

THE JURY MASTER

A NOVEL

ROBERT DUGONI

THE JURY MASTER

Author: Robert Dugonni
Page count: 448
ISBN: 978-0446578691
Formats: Hardcover, Paperback, ebook, audio
Find the author:
www.robertdugoni.com

*#8 National Independent
Booksellers List*

In a courtroom, David Sloane can grab a jury and make it dance. He can read jurors' expressions, feel their emotions, know their thoughts. With this remarkable ability, Sloane gets juries to believe the unbelievable, excuse the inexcusable, and return the most astonishing verdicts. The only barrier to Sloane's professional success is his conscience—until he gets a call from a man later found dead, and his life rockets out of control.

Reviews:

John Grisham, move over. With his debut courtroom thriller, *The Jury Master,* Seattle author Robert Dugoni explodes from the tired pack of Grisham wannabes with a riveting tale of murder, treachery and skullduggery at the highest levels.

—*Seattle Times*

Dugoni is well out in front ... a writer to watch.

—*Kirkus*

This thriller is reminiscent of the early John Grisham and should easily find its way onto the best sellers lists.

—*Library Journal*

A rapid-fire fictional debut. The action keeps coming, so omnivorous thrill seekers who favor Martini and Grisham may want to give Dugoni a look.

—*Booklist*

With tense courtroom action & intense legal suspense *The Jury Master* proves, to put it mildly, to be an astounding read. Through the protagonist, the suave, debonair attorney David Sloane, the author delivers a punching legal thriller.

—*RebeccasReads*

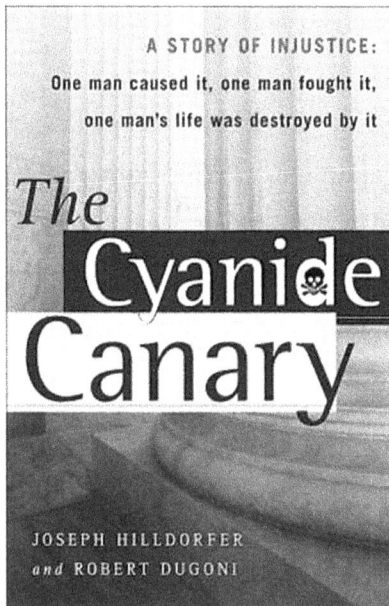

THE CYANIDE CANARY

Author: Robert Dugonni
Page count: 352
ISBN: 978-0743246521
Formats: Hardcover, Paperback, audio
Find the author: www. robertdugoni.com

Washington Post Best Book of the Year Selection
Idaho Book of the Year

The Cyanide Canary is the riveting true story of a horrific crime—of a brave young man left for dead, an unscrupulous business mogul, and the relentless EPA investigator who fought to overcome injustice.

On a crisp summer morning in Soda Springs, Idaho, twenty-year-old Scott Dominguez kissed his fiancée goodbye and went to work for Allan Elias, the owner of Evergreen Resources, an enter-prise Dominguez thought was in the business of producing fertil-izer from mining waste. A for-mer high school wrestler blessed with Tom Cruise-like good looks, Dominguez seemed to have unlimited potential, but by eleven o'clock that morning he was fight-ing for his life, pulled unconscious from a cyanide-laced storage tank and not expected to live through the night.

In Seattle, Special Agent Joseph Hilldorfer of the Environmental Protection Agency was given the job of finding out what happened to Dominguez and why. Initially Hilldorfer did not want the case, still frustrated by an intense two-year investigation that concluded with corporate polluters walk-ing out of a federal courthouse free. But as he learned more, Hilldorfer, the son of a Pittsburgh cop with a blue-collar work ethic, was touched by Scott's suffer-ing and outraged at Elias's cal-lous disregard for his employees' well-being.

Hilldorfer and his partner, Special Agent Bob Wojnicz, joined forces with seasoned Boise Assistant U.S. Attorney George Breitsameter and an indefati-gable, brilliant young attorney from the Department of Justice's Environmental Crimes Section named David Uhlmann. Together they would uncover the horrify-ing truths and build the criminal case against Elias.

A former New York whiz kid and Arizona real estate and busi-ness mogul, Elias owned busi-nesses that had polluted Idaho with hazardous waste for nearly a decade. Yet Elias never spent a single day in jail, openly boasted of beating the environmental quality regulations, and avoided any significant fines. Would this case be any different?

Hilldorfer, Uhlmann, and the government trial team embarked on an epic courtroom battle that would stretch them to the limits. What began as a struggle for jus-tice for one young man became a fight by the EPA for its very abil-ity to enforce the nation's envi-ronmental laws and to bring environmental polluters to jus-tice. In the balance was whether Allan Elias would ever spend a day in jail.

Gripping, powerful, and com-pulsively readable, *The Cyanide Canary* is a major achievement in the classic tradition of "A Civil Action," a book that unfolds like fiction yet is alarmingly true.

Reviews:

The Cyanide Canary is often is bone-chilling in its intensity and in the facts it reveals. This is a startling chronicle of just how far some businesses will go in pursuit of profit and how little regard they have for the safety or well-being of their employees. Caution: This book will make you angry.

—*Oregon Statesman Journal*

The Cyanide Canary is a marvelously suspenseful tale...a bona fide thriller pitting joyous, decent good guys against a villain without a scintilla of redeeming social value. Who wins in this robust scenario? Read the book and find out.

—*Washington Post*

...An electrically charged narrative... A top-notch nonfiction legal thriller.

—*Kirkus Starred Review*

An enthralling legal drama, evoking both outrage over worker safety and suspense over the outcome of the trial. The authors tell a fully rounded, gripping story of how environmental crime is prosecuted in the real world.

—*Booklist Starred Review*

About the author Robert Dugoni

A writer turned lawyer turned writer, Robert Dugoni was born in Pocatello, Idaho and raised in Burlingame, California. Growing up the middle child in a family of ten siblings, Dugoni jokes that he didn't get much of a chance to talk, so he wrote. By the seventh grade he knew he wanted to be a writer.

Dugoni wrote his way to Stanford University, receiving writing awards along the way, and majored in communications/journalism and creative writing while working as a reporter for the Stanford Daily. He graduated Phi Beta Kappa and worked briefly as a reporter in the Metro Office and the San Gabriel Valley Office of the Los Angeles Times.

Dugoni attended the UCLA law school and practiced law for 13 years in San Francisco. His longing to return to writing never wavered, however, and in 1999 he awoke one morning and made the decision to quit law and write novels. On the 4-year anniversary of his wedding day, he drove a U-Haul trailer across the Oregon-Washington border and settled in Seattle to pursue his dreams.

For the next three years, Dugoni worked daily in an 8 foot by 8 foot windowless office in Pioneer Square to complete three novels, winning the 1999 and 2000 Pacific Northwest Writer's Conference Literary Contests.

For more on Robert Dugoni and his novels, visit his website at www.robertdugonni.com

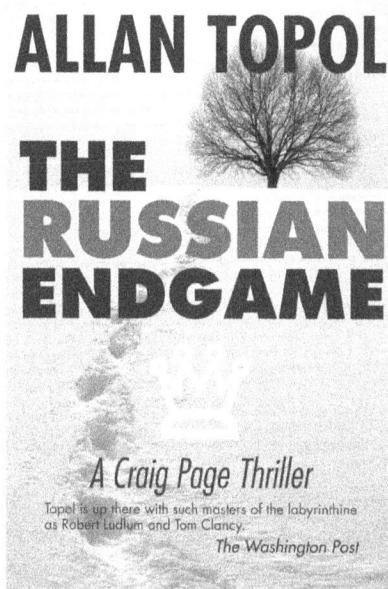

Title: *The Russian Endgame*
Author: Alan Topol
Page count: 328
ASIN: 978-1590799994
Formats: Paperback, ebook
Find the author:
www.allantopol.com
Star rating: ★ ★ ★ ★ ★

REVIEW BY FRAN LEWIS

OVERVIEW

The third in the trilogy again features the daring Craig Page and gutsy Elizabeth Crowder. Once again they do battle with the ruthless Chinese General Zhou, who joins forces with Russian President Kuznov to form an alliance, which will inflict damage on the United States and Europe.

Following on the heels of *The China Gambit* and *Spanish Revenge*, national bestselling author, Allan Topol, returns with *The Russian Endgame*. This time he offers a riveting conclusion to a dangerous three-part game of international conspiracy, politics, and greed.

When former KGB agent Dimitri Orlov orchestrates an alliance between two world powers bent on domination, he unleashes a powerful chain of events that will rock the Western World. The agenda? Eliminate the president of the United States and seize classified military weaponry capable of shifting the balance of world power.

But before this nefarious scheme can reach fruition, Craig Page, joined by Elizabeth Crowder, is on the scene, ready to confront a painful past and the enemies that helped create it. But can the indomitable director of counterterrorism emerge victorious?

Finding himself facing an old enemy unexpectedly catapulted into a lethal position of power, Craig is pushed to the limit in an effort to foil his enemy's deadly plans and keep potentially devastating military technology out of the hands of those prepared to destroy the world as he knows it.

REVIEWS:

Topol is up there with such masters of the labyrinthine as Robert Ludlum and Tom Clancy.
—*The Washington Post*

John Grisham and Richard North Patterson may have a new successor
—*Publishers Weekly*

Topol creates believable characters with real problems and emotions; he constructs a tight, suspenseful plot that has us flipping pages as fast as we can find out what happens while we root 100% for a hero we don't altogether like.
—*The Los Angeles Times*

Takes off at warp speed... Topol has done his homework.
—*Washingtonian Online On Conspiracy*

Topol's fiction is woven from the threads of real events and real-life concerns.
—*Legal Times on Dark Ambition*

Power: the ability to influence the actions or behavior of people. Authority is often the word used for power. Power can be evil or unjust but the exercise of power is accepted as endemic to humans as social beings. Bosses try wielding their power and sometimes strong-arm employees into doing their bidding or creating unfair conditions at work. Some company bigwigs use their influences to intimidate their subordinates. But, how far will someone go in order to gain control of a nation or to become more powerful to those running a nation? One man decides he wants to be the second in power of a dominant nation. When former KGB agent Dmitri Orlov puts his mind to something he often thinks he has the entire plan perfectly created, each nuance figured out and hopefully will gain the respect of some powerful people. But, not everything goes as planned as he will learn.

Breaking into the home of the president of Russia, Orlov hopes to gain his interest in a plan he has to convince the head of the military of China to align with Russia to become the two most dominate powers in the world. But, what he does is set off a time bomb so deadly that it unleashes more than just a chain of horrific events that changes the dynamic of the United States. Meeting with Chairman Zhou after gaining permission from the Russian president, he hopes to convince him of his loyalty to Russia, the power he has been given from the president of his country, and his hope of protecting his sister, who happens to be the chairman's mistress. But, plans are not always created or carried out the way you want and alliances are formed, but when you are not quite up to speed and can be dominated the end result is you might get hung out to dry. Dealing with Zhou proves to be dangerous for Orlov in many ways. Zhou is power hungry and wants anyone that might be in his way eliminated, starting with President Dalton of the United States. Demanding that Orlov prove his honesty and loyalty to the mission and gain his trust, Zhou has enlisted him to kill our president. Not sure how to go about

this, he relates the information to the Russian president, who seems to have the contacts and the know how to tell him how to get the job done. With the aid of a pilot and several others, he manages to get the job done, mirroring the incident to the assassination of Kennedy.

Craig Paige has had a total fixation with Chairman Zhou since he ordered the death of his daughter Francesca, and he aims to take him down no matter what it takes. Power: Just how far will he use his in order to get the job done? But, there is so much more as the president is eliminated, and Orlov thinks he is home free and hopes to set up a meeting between both presidents. But Zhou throws him another dangerous curve ball as author Alan Topol takes readers inside the mind of a mad man who is so hungry for power, wants to become the next president of China, and has created and set in motion a plan that will send shock waves around the world. A second stipulation is thrown at Orlov as he is told that he will now have to steal the PGS classified military weaponry program and make sure it gets in the hands of China in order to give them the edge militarily over the United States. Prompt Global Strike: Powerful, created by five brilliant engineers, and dangerous in the wrong hands.

The Chinese president is still steaming, his Operation Dragon Oil mission foiled, and the fact that anyone would try to compete with him for the presidency. Mei Ling is quite powerful in government, and although the primary candidate for the position, Zhou managed to corrupt the military, get rid of anyone in his way, and make sure they would not survive or get in the way of what he wanted to do,

But before this nefarious scheme can reach fruition, Craig Page is on the scene, joined by companion Elizabeth Crowder, ready to confront a painful past and the enemies that helped create it. But can the indomitable director of counterterrorism emerge victorious? Finding himself facing an old enemy unexpectedly catapulted into a lethal position of power,

Craig is pushed to the limit in an effort to foil his enemy's deadly plans and keep potentially devastating military technology out of the hands of the Zhou. But, things get out of hand and the Russian KGB agent uses some tricks of his own to blackmail one of the engineers into giving him the discs with the information he needs. What happens next will definitely change the dynamics of his plan as the engineer pulls a switch of his own and the unexpected happens.

When the missions on both sides fail and Craig is no closer to finding Orlov and stopping Zhou in his tracks, he decides to take matters in a different direction. Now appointed as the director of the CIA by the new president, he has the resources and power at his fingertips; but does he have the know how to get the job done? As the bait is flaunted in the face of the Russian agent, things do not turn out exactly the way he expects.

Lives are at stake, the president is counting on Craig, but his rogue behavior endangers many and lives are lost because his reasoning falls short and his obsession to get Zhou wins out. Just how far will he go to win? Just how far will Orlov sacrifice his sister and her safety to get what he wants? Power: sometimes it is stronger than an aphrodisiac (an agent (as a food or drug) that arouses or is held to arouse sexual desire). Three men possessed with a goal, each stopping at nothing to succeed. Will Craig stop what he knows Zhou has planned? Will Orlov succeed in helping him get the technology and if he does what's next? Pawns in the master plan, just who will say "Checkmate" before it's all said and done, and who will lose it all in a game of chance?

As we hear the many players engage in different conversations and hear Craig at the task force meeting, one-man leaks it all and another is found to be a traitor to our country. But, the final endgame will change more than just what so many tried to put in motion. Depleting the U.S. of its oil resources, betrayals, deceit, double dipping, double crosses, and one man determined to avenge his daughter's death at all cost. But, just what is Craig's endgame? An ending so explosive and a final outcome that will change the course of events of three nations as Craig Page, Elizabeth Crowder, and teams from many other countries search for the evidence to bring down one man who just wants POWER! Will he avenge his daughter's death? What about the fate of Orlov, and what will happen when the truth about his sister comes to light? Just how will this all end? Sometimes a split second makes all the difference. Sometimes we find a way to create reason when there is only doubt. A decision that would definitely decide just whose Endgame is victorious. Author Alan Topol creates more than just a moral issue, ethical judgment and final scenes that will leave many unanswered questions and make readers wonder what is next for the new CIA director. Once again author Alan Topol raises the bar for other thriller authors to follow as Craig Page, rogue, impulsive, creative, and always two steps ahead of himself and everyone else, works his magic to bring down one man. Power: wait until you read the ending before you decide where it falls.

BOOK REVIEWS

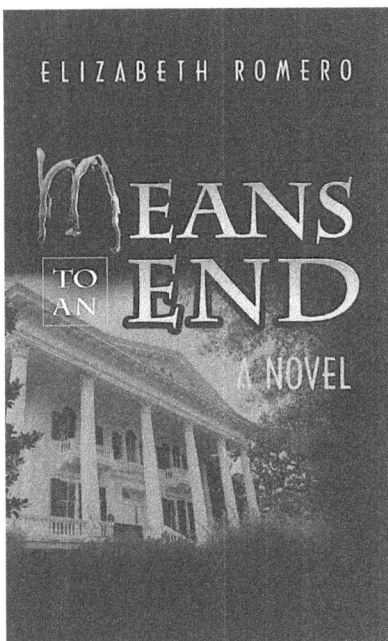

MEANS TO AN END

Author: Elizabeth Romero
Page count: 356
ISBN: 978-1-62652-041-7
Formats: Paperback, ebook
Find the author:

www.ElizabethRomeroBooks.com

Star rating: ★★★★★

REVIEW BY FRAN LEWIS

Two women whose lives are bound together will never find their way to freedom as Marie Broudreaux pays a heavy price for one mistake that her family will never forgive. Imagine a round cage of iron and sitting within the confines of this cage with limited resources, little money, and no means of escape. Like with a circus master or slave owner, you are treated to frequent beatings and abuse at the hand of the master or owner because you failed to meet their standards or because they felt like venting their anger on you.

Ashby Devereaux lived her life in fear of her stepfather Garrett who reveled in torching her and her mother with his temper and brute force. Married to Garrett, Marie Broudreaux, after her father literally sold her into bondage for being pregnant with twins, paid a heavy price for her one big mistake.

Cruelty seemed to make him feel like a man, and abusing Ashby and her brother Danny seemed to be his way of releasing his anger and tension. Drunk, a thief, and not worth much of anything, he wielded his intensions on his stepdaughter without any regard for the consequences or her feelings. But, one incident in school and one teacher would change it all and possibly give her the courage she needed to stand up to this man and much more.

Mrs. Bass seemed to realize that Ashby was enduring something at home but would not divulge anything to her or anyone else. When chosen to be Queen of the Carnival at school, she realized that she would be the brunt of many insults of the popular girls because of her poor economic background and their enjoyment at being cruel. A young man named Bobby would change how she felt about herself, but one incident would take it all away. With nowhere to turn at times and a mother who was addicted to drugs, always out of it, and could barely hold her head up, this poor young girl living in the backwoods mountains of North Carolina had to fend for herself and pray for her own salvation.

When Garrett was arrested and did a stint in jail, she looked at this as a positive sign. But a man named Johnny Mac, her stepfather's friend, wanted to use her as collateral or payment for a debt he claimed Garrett owed him. Ashby had changed and something within her fired her up, and she would no longer allow anyone to use her for a punching bag or intimate fun. Where could she go and how would she escape his wrath? Finding something in her barn allowed her the freedom she might need to leave and leave something for her mother to live on. But before she had the chance to go she revealed something to her mother about Garrett, the incident turned ugly, and the result would send her far away from her home, never to return. As the cage began to open and Ashby might finally be free, something within her held her back. Could she leave her mother to clean up the mess she created?

Ashby headed to New Orleans to find her grandparents and learn more about the stories her mother shared with her, and maybe connect with her long gone brother. Would the law come after her? Could she hide from her past by changing who she was in the present? Would reinventing herself change who she really was? Could she hide forever? Finding herself all alone on the streets of New Orleans, she was befriended by someone who directed her to a rooming house and hopefully a job. Oversleeping got her fired, but another job came to light as she moved to The Smoking House, where she could either become one of the working girls or a maid. Opting to become a maid and befriended by Ms. Blanche, the proprietor, she drew the attention of a local judge whose heart she seemed to have captivated. Given the option of remaining with Ms. Blanche

or moving in with the judge, a friend advised her as to what would keep her safe.

Getting to know the judge and wanting to please him kept Monique/Ashby content. But, in the back of her mind she knew that someone was after her and that the law might catch up with her, and the result could change things for her forever. Never thinking that the judge might know about her past or that this could be a setup from the start, she moved into his home, was befriended by Corinne, his maid and cook, and the rest still remained to be seen. Abuse never leaves you, and the fear of being with any man still gave her the chills.

As Monique/Ashby gets to know Bradley, the undertone within their relationship allows readers to know that smooth sailing is not in the cards for them. He enlisted the help of someone to learn more about her; but why? While she became more comfortable within her surroundings, closer to Bradley she still had the fear of being found out.

When the pieces of the intricate story started taking shape and formed a pattern that sent the authorities in Monique's direction, she overheard a conversation and decided to run away once more. With the help of her friend Bebet she hoped to remain hidden and safe, but when Bradley forced both of their hands what would the outcome be? With Danny now in the picture and the hope of learning more about her past, what happens when she hears Marie's words will surprise the reader as the truth comes to light.

One young girl living in fear for her life and afraid to confide in anyone, even the one man she claimed to love. Garrett was more than just an abusive and evil man…he did things that would have brought the law down on him had someone not taken matters into their own hands first. When families were torn apart their lives could not be sewn back together, but one man was determined to give Monique the life he felt she so greatly deserved.

What is the fate of this young girl? Will the truth about Garrett's death ever come out? What were Marie's final words? When a parent cannot protect her children, what happens will bring tears to the reader's eyes when one startling revelation is revealed. An ending that is so filled with unexpected twists and surprises, and a young girl whose life will never be the same. The epilogue moves ahead and we learn about her future, and hope the author will bring Monique Boudreaux back again. Sometimes we do things in order to create what some might say is the only way to survive, or a *Means to An End*! This is one novel that brings to light what happens when secrets are kept, fear is instilled, abuse of many types are inflicted on so many, and the end result can be tragic. Just what Monique does and where she is now you will have to learn for yourself. Will she wind up with Bradley and turn her life around? The answers to those questions fill the final pages of this five star novel, and you will have to read it to find out. Let's hope the metal cage door opens and never closes again.

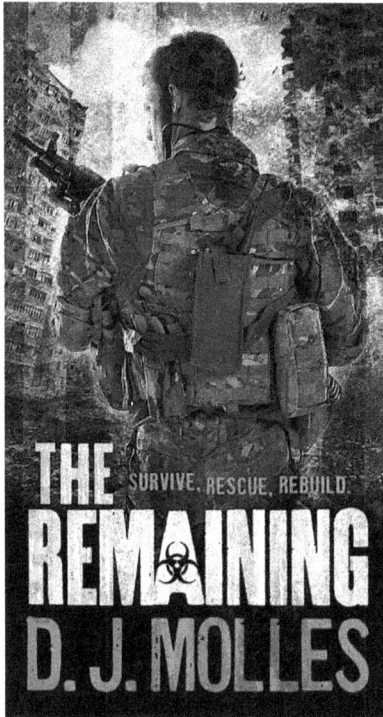

THE REMAINING

Author: D.J. Molles
Page count: 352
ISBN: 978-0316404150
Formats: Paperback, ebook, audio book
Find the author on Facebook

Star rating: ★ ★ ★ ★ ★

The world as he knows it comes to an end while Lee Harden is sequestered in "the hole" awaiting communication from his US government superiors. Lee is one of 48 "coordinators" trained and safeguarded by the government and tasked with resurrecting the good old US of A should the world as we know it come to an end.

Lee isn't the best at following the rules, and breaks out of his secure bunker before the 30-day quarantine period has expired. When he steps off his front porch, a teenaged zombie attacks him and nearly ends the story before it begins. Once the zombie is dispatched, Lee decides to check on his neighbors and thus begins his odyssey.

As the story progresses, you can't help but cheer for the hapless hero as he makes his fair share of mistakes along the way and takes his knocks because of them. Even though he has his faults, Lee is a good guy through and through, and a truly decent human being. The author, on the other hand, is absolutely ruthless with is characters, sometimes to the point that all you can think is "geez, give this poor guy a break!" when the bullets are flying and the zombies are beating on the door.

The storyline is captivating and the well-developed characters are faced with new challenges around every corner. The book is professionally written and edited, the story flows well and all of the characters elicit an emotional response (both good and bad) from the reader. It is also a nice twist on the zombie genre, since the zombies can reason up to a point, which makes things interesting for the characters who have to combat them. It's hard to believe that this book was originally self-published.

If you love books about the zombie apocalypse, a strong, nearly indestructible hero and adrenaline-pumping adventure, then this is the book (and series) for you! Books in the series include: *The Remaining, The Remaining: Aftermath, The Remaining: Refugees, The Remaining: Fractured* (Book 5 in the series, *The Remaining: Faith,* is halfway done, according to the author!)

REVIEW BY ROBIN SURFACE

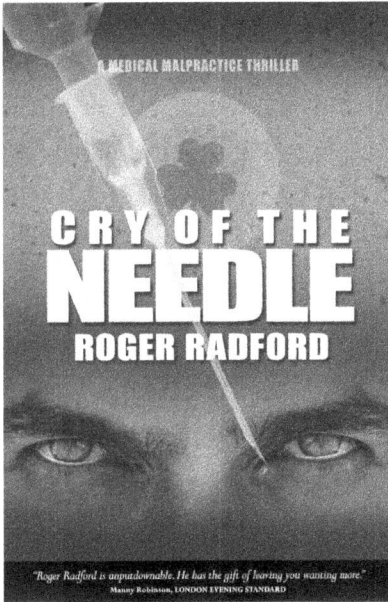

CRY OF THE NEEDLE

Author: Roger Radford
Page count: 287
Formats: eBook

Star rating: ★ ★ ★ ★ ★

What a brilliant thriller this is! However, it is much more. It is an education on medical malpractice and consequent cover-ups by the pharmaceutical giants of which the author has first hand knowledge (see author's note at end of book).

The scene is London when Teresa Kelly has an epidural that goes wrong during the birth of her fourth child. Already you are gripped with anger that matches that of her Irish husband Kieran Kelly as he watches his wife in agony. Kieran was once a hit man for the Provisional IRA's internal affairs, now leading a life of relative anonymity after leaving his native Belfast.

The consequences of this medical error are far reaching, taking us on a journey that evokes many emotions. We follow Kieran Kelly on his voyage of discovery about arachnoiditis, a disease caused by malpractice. How he plots revenge. How he eventually meets up with the remarkable and courageous Countess Magda von Esterhazy, a sufferer of this awful disease, who understands his feelings.

At the same time we have a sub plot with Jonathan Tring, a scientist working for a pharmaceutical company hoping to expose the corruption of his powerful boss, Jack Proctor. Will Jonathan be able to succeed? What happens when he meets Fiona?

What part does the enigmatic Sharon, Jack Proctor's beautiful wife, play?

What about corruption in the government? Will they continue to keep their heads in the sand?

There is so much to this story, but in spite of the many angles it is still fast paced. I wanted to leave all my chores and other responsibilities and just keep on reading, especially as the thrilling, edge of seat climax approaches

In spite of knowing what Kieran Kelly planned was wrong, part of you is willing him on.

This is one of the best books I have ever read. A very powerful and compelling story, which brings many emotions to the fore.

I strongly recommend *Cry of the Needle* as a must read.

REVIEW BY ANN STANMORE

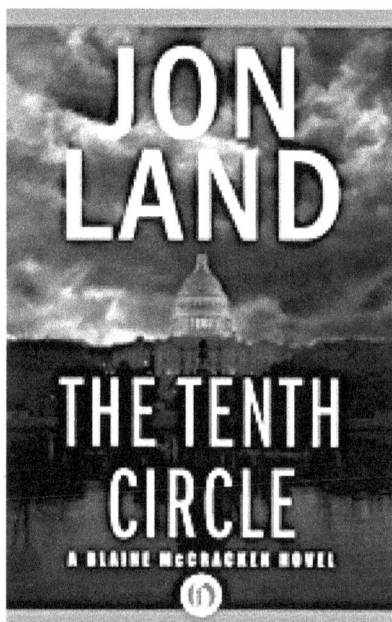

THE TENTH CIRCLE

Author: Jon Land
Page count: 536
ISBN: 978-1480414792
Formats: Paperback, ebook

Star rating: ★★★★★

REVIEW BY FRAN LEWIS

McCracken's back! And I couldn't be happier. Jon Land's *The Tenth Circle* is a knockout thriller blending history, cutting-edge science, and nonstop action. Ancient mysteries, ghost ships, and a modern threat like no other...this is a novel that grips you by the throat and refuses to let go until the last page.

—*James Rollins, New York Times bestselling author of* The Eye Of God

Jon Land is one hell of a writer. His vivid recreations of the past, his characterizations and his nonstop ticking clock tension had me turning the pages so fast they were smoldering. I really loved this book.

—*Peter James, #1 International Bestselling author of* Dead Man's Time

Blaine McCracken is capable of making things happen. Entering a nuclear facility, learning about its inner workings and seeing the capabilities behind the locked doors would make most shudder and send chills down their spine, but not Blaine. As he takes on the role of famous photographer and passes the many checkpoints within the Iranian facility, his camera flashes the shots, takes down each scene, and hopefully will help tell a story that will wake up the world; but first he has to avoid detection. Even the best laid plans do not always result in the answers and results you want, and Blaine's natural instincts kick in, his realities of the situation come to light, and he realizes that in order to complete his task he will have to do more than just pretend. With those in charge proud of their accomplishments, explaining that their target is Israel and that they're hoping to wipe her out and make her just a distant memory, Blaine's snap decisions and fast and hard reactions would let the Iranian's know that dealing with Blaine would be anything but what they expected. How he pulls off his escape and what happens to those within the locked and secured walls you will learn for yourself with the explosive solution that will rock more than just the nuclear plant.

We meet Reverend Jeremiah Rule, who is a threat to humanity, devoid of morals and feelings, and whose behavior is inflammatory, hoping to rid the world of every Muslim person, sect burning, one Koran at a time. Inciting many terrorist attacks throughout many cities and towns, this twisted man is not working alone to create this havoc. Rising to his pulpit, he brings his flock to a frenzy asking them to sacrifice something near and dear to them and place it within the fire he ignites.

There are nine circles of hell, and a tenth one that when unfurled is "a lost canto of Dante's Inferno—what appears to be the tenth circle of Hell. The ninth circle was previously understood to be the lowest point of Hell reached by Dante and his guide Virgil before ascending on their journey toward Paradise. A portion of the 14th-century manuscript, translated into English prose, is reproduced below." *The Tenth Circle*: One that is for those who have lied to themselves, pretend to hurt the ones they love and deserve. Who is behind Jeremiah Rule and why is he so powerful? Where does his support come from, and why is he able to spiral out of control? The author brings one little boy to the altar to sacrifice something precious, and relates an incident so horrific from Rule's past it will make you shudder as the death of one young child brings to light the kindness he pretends to the one in the present when the flames roar and his image is illuminated.

Listening to Rule and the one man working with him, we learn more about his corruption, taking money from his followers you understand that he is receiving support from someone else, and their power together will create what they call the Tenth Circle, inflicting it on the hopeless and the damned. But, Blaine is concerned about Roanoke Island and what the connection is to the present. The author brings back our marijuana smoking Captain Seven, who enlightens not only readers but Blaine to a horrible

truth about what might have happened to those colonists, and what impact it will have on the present.

Roanoke Island is a colony in 1590 where our story begins, and the author flashes back to how but not why this colony disappears and what happens to those living there. Ralph Lane is made governor of this island and the Indians and natives begin to get along. But, not everyone welcomes the settlers, and Sir Francis Drake stops at this colony and leaves fifteen men to protect the British claim. But, when Grenville arrives, the settlement is empty, leaving the fifteen men. Next, a group of settlers arrive on July 22, 1587 with 117 people led by John White. Settling in and trying to become friends with the Croatoan tribe, although facing hostilities from others, one man is killed and other incidents happen that alert the settlers that their new home might not be safe. A supply ship returns to find not one living person three years later. No sign of war, battle, famine or even dead bodies; no sign of anything until someone sees the houses dismantled, the fort that surrounded the settlement, and the word CROATOAN carved on a post and the letters CRO on a tree.

What does it mean? Were they under the protection of the tribe? No crosses anywhere, no dangers seen, and yet no search was ever made of Croatoan Island, and this word comes haunting Blaine in the present.

Next we learn about the freighter the Mary Celeste, whose crew and passengers disappear without a trace in 1872. Why and how? Just what was hidden within their cargo hold that the author allows readers to bare knowledge of that if not found and destroyed would destroy the world? How do they link together, and what bearing do they have in the present?

When Blake, Captain Seven, and Johnny Wareagle decide to visit Roanoke Island they meet a young man named Jacob, a descendant of the Croatoan tribe, and what they uncover is not only explosive in nature but the hidden reason behind what really happened to the colonists. We meet Zarrin, who spent her childhood in a Palestinian Camp hoping to find her way to freedom. Taking piano lessons and wanting to help her teacher get his medication, she learns some hard and fast lessons when trying to save his life and fighting for her own. Killing one man—part of the Hamsa, who ran the camp—for the much needed meds for so many, she hardly copes with the brutal death of her teacher and then is taken away, sent to skill and becomes a hired assassin, but for which side? In the present we meet her and learn of her skill to mesmerize audiences with her expert piano playing, while eliminating enemies and dealing with a debiliting illness.

McCracken becomes the wanted man and he fights his way across many different continents, countries, and places to stop what is so vividly described as the "Tenth Circle of Hell." With Seven and Johnny at his side, and homeland security watching his every move, just who else wants him eliminated? Throughout the novel author Jon Land shares his expert research into the disappearance of the colonists and how the Mary Celeste's cargo ties in. What would happen if what was left in the cargo was not alcohol as stated in the ship's manifest but something more deadly? What if the terrorist attacks that have been unleashed were connected to using this weapon of mass destruction, and this was just the beginning? What if Blaine, Zarrin, and Seven teamed up to try and stop what was about to happen? When Captain Seven relates the facts about the Mary Celeste and Blaine explains the tie in to the cargo and just who these terrorists really are, you realize that someone higher up in our government is controlling things. Why? Reverend Jeremiah Rule fits right into the picture as his flock increases, his hold over so many becomes stronger, and his part to help rid the world of Muslims comes to light in a dangerous way that will bring more than just chills to the reader. What would have happened if the crew from the Mary Celeste lived to tell it all? White death! Just what is it and how will it destroy an entire country?

Legends about the past; could the colonists' disappearance be related to the weather, an invisible force that when unleashed laid claim to the colonists?

A Palestinian assassin, a Sioux Indian, Blaine McCracken, and a weed-smoking captain join forces to stop what several have put into motion. Zarrin hears the music in her head and plays the many concertos to keep her on the move and her hands moving when fighting for her life, protecting our country, and hoping to prevent what three men want to unleash: The Tenth Circle. With the help of an old buddy pretending to be senile in a retirement home, Blaine manages to figure out what the plan is, what Rule has in mind, and who is working with him. But will he figure out how to stop what they want to unleash before the end of the presidents' State of the Union Address? Jeremiah Rule: finding his way back to God, but first he needs to reconcile the horrors he inflicted in the present. Delusional, enlisting the help of a biker gang and one man who swore his allegiance to him, the result will send not only Blaine, Zarrin, and Johnny into the flames of danger but will prove to readers just how far some will go to protect our country, fight for the future, and hopefully protect the present. An ending that only author Jon Land could create and the truth behind the deadly emissions that these assassins wanted to unleash. The Tenth Circle: If not stopped the first nine would be nothing compared to what this will do. With an ending so explosive you can feel the heat, the tension, the emotions rising as Blaine McCracken uses all of this skills, his extra lives, and his know how to hopefully stop what would be more dangerous than the Black Plague, equal if not worse than an atomic bomb, and certainly change the complexion of our country. Blaine McCracken…strong, smart, down to earth, and definitely someone you want on your side. But, introducing Zarrin added another strong female character that I hope this outstanding author brings back again.

Special Interview with Jon Land: *The Tenth Circle*

Interviewed by Mark Rubinstein

Q: *The Tenth Circle* begins with an epigraph from Ralph Waldo Emerson: "A hero is no braver than an ordinary man, but he is braver five minutes longer." How does that observation inform your protagonist, Blaine McCracken?

Wow, that's a great question right off the bat! I think the Emerson quote implies that great feats of bravery unfold in very short beats of time. And what keeps happening during those extra five minutes is basically what has come to define Blaine McCracken, particularly his ability to walk into a hostile situation and always find a way to walk out. Come to think of it, almost all the big action scenes in *The Tenth Circle* (And, man are there a lot of them!) would probably run about five real life minutes. And it's those five-minute sequences where McCracken excels the most. So the quote is more than just a figurative metaphor; it's kind of a life mantra for Blaine.

Q: Your novel takes us from sixteen-century colonial America to nineteen-century England, and from present-day Iran to a bridge in Missouri and a church in Florida, among other times and places. Please describe your research process.

Not to belittle myself but, confession time here, I am a Google fanatic. I've gotten real good at knowing what exactly to search to find what I want and it was a pretty simple process this time out since so much is known about the subjects you list above. I started the book with the notion of taking two of the greatest historical mysteries of all time and linking them together. So that's where I started my research process. I research pretty much as I go instead of in advance because I don't know what I need until I get there. The bridge in Missouri is a perfect example. So too is the description of the Reverend Rule's church, which was built to conform to a historical site in the area—more fodder from my research.

Q: McCracken is a Vietnam War veteran in his early sixties. What challenges does McCracken's age present to you in crafting a convincing thriller? Does his age also present opportunities?

First off, when I decided to resurrect McCracken first in *Pandora's Temple* and now in *The Tenth Circle*, I felt it only fair to my readers to age him chronologically in real time, as opposed to cheating his age. I actually really didn't think I had much of a choice. I'd so clearly established his Vietnam background in the first nine books in the series that it would be disingenuous to the reader not to work with his real age—hey, if I made him forty, that means he would have fighting in Vietnam at the age of ten! By the same token, though, I found this to be a terrific metaphor for what so many talented individuals of this age are experiencing today thanks to downsizing and outsourcing. When *Pandora* opens, McCracken's phone hasn't rung for a while and he's starting to wonder if it ever will again. That's all too real for too many truly talented and exceptional men and women today who are the same age. That's one of the great opportunities an older hero presents, not to mention the fact that I've been writing Blaine for twenty-eight years now, so his audience has aged with him. The biggest challenge is maintaining credibility for his exploits. Let's face it, there are some things, a lot of things, you can't do nearly as well at sixty as you can at even forty. But sixty, as they say, is kind of the new forty. So it's important to establish how Blaine's still able to pull this stuff off and not put him in situations that would be considered ridiculous for a person his age.

Q: Among the fascinating characters in the novel is Zarrin, a world-renowned classical pianist. However, music is only one of her talents. Do you have plans for her in future stories?

No, I don't, but I love that you asked! See, the key to making any book like this work is to create a supporting cast just as interesting as the primary players. They need to be fleshed out and developed in a way that endears them to the reader and distinguishes them from other foils in both my books and others. So the fact that you posed the question tells me *The Tenth Circle* left you wanting to see more of Zarrin and that's the most important test when it comes to whether a character works or not.

Q: In the past, McCracken has been able to successfully navigate his violent world by avoiding personal attachments. In the *The Tenth Circle,* he's formed one that nearly leads to disaster. What interests you about the conflict between McCracken's service for the greater good and his need to form emotional bonds with others?

Another great question and one that could be applied to my Caitlin Strong character as well, if not better! It's a delicate mix between making him seem too vulnerable while providing a strong emotional stake in the action for him. The question you've raised here goes to the heart of McCracken's complexity as a character as well as a comic book type superhero. Especially in these more recent entries, *Pandora's Temple* and *The Tenth Circle*, with McCracken turning sixty and starting to question some of his choices. It's not enough for me to have him skate unscarred both physically and emotionally through this adventure and the next one. Conflict is far, far more effective when it's personal and suspense is also better done when the hero is racing to save someone who is important to them. So I don't necessary think there's a conflict between McCracken's service to the greater good and his need to bond. I think they're intrinsi-

cally connected. His service is what defines him and it's on those terms that enable him to seek out those who help make him understand who he is and why he does what he does, even after all these years.

Q: You've written other series—for example, your series featuring Texas Ranger Caitlyn Strong. You brought Blaine McCracken back in 2012's *Pandora's Temple* after a fourteen-year hiatus. What inspires you to continue the story of a particular protagonist?

I realized there was more to do with him. I'd grown and so had he and, more to the point, the action-adventure thriller has made a huge comeback in recent years, so the timing was perfect—also for two other reasons. First, Open Road Media, publisher of *The Tenth Circle*, had brought out five earlier titles in the series and they performed so well that bringing McCracken back in a new book was a natural. Second, it helped that I was kind of auditioning to be one of Clive Cussler's co-authors and had written a lengthy sample of a book that would later become *Pandora*. The bad news is that becoming a Cussler co-author simply wasn't the right fit for me. The good news is that adapting the material to better suit my own style led to McCracken's return, which very well may never have happened otherwise.

Q: *The Tenth Circle* has been published as an eBook original. What's your take on the "print vs. digital" debate and whether new technology is good or bad for authors?

First off, anything that gets books into the hands of readers is a good thing. I don't see the print vs. digital thing as a debate so much a struggle between reading preferences. It's funny because Open Road Media, publisher of *The Tenth Circle*, has an entirely different marketing philosophy than Forge, the company that publishes my Caitlin Strong thrillers, a whole different model. All this new technology is mostly very good for writers, since books no longer need ever go out of print and newer titles have longer to catch on the digital world than the print world. The downside is that, with consolidation in the industry and loss of so many bookstores, the increase in my digital sales doesn't even come close to approaching the sales I've lost in paperback and even hardcovers. This is a bestseller-driven business and the digital world, unfortunately or not, has actually driven that trend even farther.

Q: Who are some of your favorite *non-thriller*/mystery writers? How have they influenced your writing, it at all?

Uh-oh, you're really challenging me now! Well, that's a tough one. I'd have to go back to my college days at Brown and reading the likes of Hemingway, Faulkner, Fitzgerald, Nathaniel West, Charles Dickens. Notice I didn't mention Shakespeare because at heart, he WAS a thriller writer and so were Hemingway and Dickens to a great extent. But one of the tools I think I learned from reading so-called serious fiction was ambiguity, how their conflicted characters, and heroes in particular, are drawn in shades of gray instead of being presented in black and white. I think when we strive for that in thriller fiction, we end up with material that's much more ambitious and original as opposed to formulaic, which is a big problem in our genre today. With so many thrillers to contend with in the marketplace, it's especially important to distinguish yourself and that's what presenting your characters in an ambiguous vein provides.

Q: The clichéd piece of advice for aspiring writers is "write what you know." In *The Tenth Circle*, you write about Colonial America, France under Napoleon III, present-day Boston, the Israeli secret service, hidden nuclear missile sites, classical piano, religious fanaticism, and futuristic engineering. Would you describe that as "writing what you

know?" More generally, could you describe your writing process?

Writing what you know is the worst advice a writer can possibly be given, because no one can know enough to write as many books as I've written. The simple fact of the matter is that a big-scale thriller like *Pandora's Temple* is literally packed with all kinds of information about technology, locations, history, weaponry. No one could possibly know everything you need to about so many things to write a book like this. All I can say is thank God for Google! It makes all writers technological rock stars because in a book like this you don't have to be perfect, but you certainly need to be credible and convincing. As far as my own practice goes, I am the anti-outliner. I believe in spontaneity and trusting my characters to guide me where they want, and need, to go. When I start a book, I know the general plot but not how it's going to end precisely. I'm usually about a hundred pages ahead in my mind, but that's it. Here's the way I look at it: if I don't know what's going to happen next, the reader can't possibly know. The problem, at least in my last two books, has been that the first drafts just weren't very good. But, like in sports, it doesn't matter how you start, it's how you finish and I think *The Tenth Circle* finished up great.

Q: Tell us about your next project.

It's my next Caitlin Strong book, *Strong Darkness*. Six weeks ago, with all the praise *Strong Rain Falling* has been getting, I was facing the terrible reality that it just wasn't as good a book as that one. Now, three rewrites later, I'm happy to report that the book looks great and I think will be very well received by the millions of Caitlin fans out there—well, thousands maybe; make that hundreds (laughs) but, hey, it leaves me lots of room for growth!

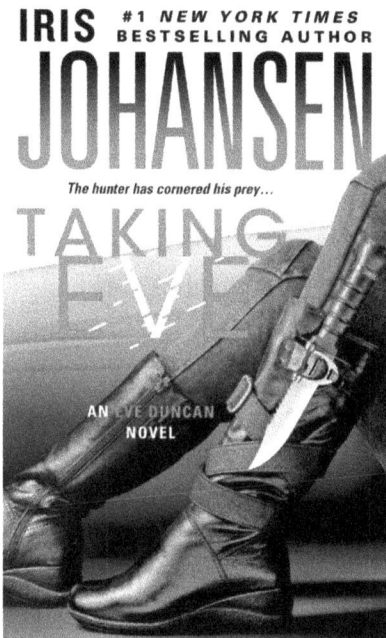

TAKING EVE

Iris Johansen

Page Count: 432 pages

Price: $27.00 U.S./$29.00 CAN.

ISBN: 978-0-345-52654-0

Formats: paperback, hardcover, eBook, audio

Find the Author: Goodreads

Star rating: ★ ★ ★ ★ ★

GoodReads Review: Someone is so desperate to get Eve services that he will do anything to get them. Once the reconstruction is done then what. Is this the last of Eve?

Taking Eve is one of those books that will keep you reading long past your bedtime. There is plenty of action to go around through out the book and it will keep the reader wondering what's next.

Thoroughly enjoyed the return of Jane McGuire and the introduction of Margaret, a 19-year-old with a secret past and some interesting skills.

There is also a secret revealed that may shock you but that will only make you want to read *Hunting Eve and Silencing Eve* that are soon to be released during the holidays and in the new year.

Taking Eve is a definite five star read that deserved bonus points for the creepiness factor of the new villain in town.

REVIEW BY KAREN VAUGHN

RECOMMENDED READING

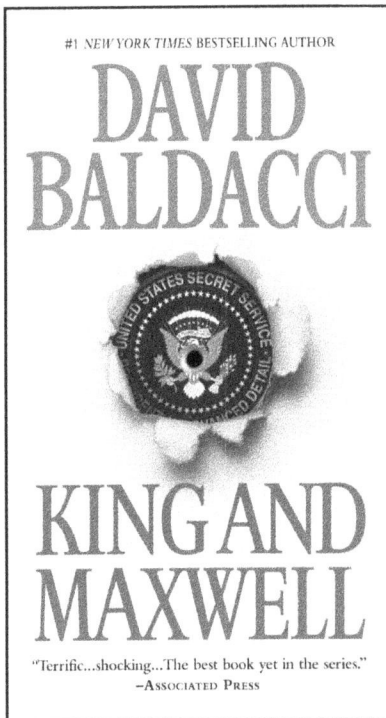

KING AND MAXWELL
David Baldacci
Page Count: 448 pages
ISBN: 978-0-345-52654-0
Formats: paperback, hardcover, eBook, audio

Star rating: ★★★★★

REVIEW BY FRAN LEWIS

Sam Wingo is on a mission and something goes wrong. Sent to Afghanistan and meeting with men whom he thinks are CIA, the result will do more than put him in danger. As the mission fails and the truth behind these men comes out, he calls his commanding officer to be told he'd better come in. But, the knowledge of what the army tells his family is shocking, revealing a cover up that would tear him and his young son apart. Tyler Wingo is a teenage boy caught in the web of lies and deceits that have been handed to him. Homeland Security agents— so they say—, police, army officers, and detectives are all hot on his trail making sure that he does not pursue finding out what really happened to his father. But, when Tyler learns the truth that his father, a soldier, was killed in action in Afghanistan, one single text would change it all and send him on a path that would change many lives.

Before taking out the GPS and battery of his phone and after disconnecting with his commanding officer, Sam Wingo sends one final message. Sean King and Michelle Maxwell own their own private investigating firm and Tyler hires them to find out what happened to his father until he fires them and changes his mind. Looking into the case after finding Tyler running through the rain and angry when told about his father's death, Sean and Michelle become embroiled in the teenager's life, not expecting the obstacles, snags, and silence they receive from the army and the police. Just why don't they want them to find out what happened to Sam?

Author David Baldacci takes readers inside the battle zone along with Sam as he treks his way through Jalalabad, Khyber Pakhtunkhwa, Afghanistan, hoping to reach New Delhi, including the history behind the Taliban, Al-Qaida, and the many reasons why Sam is being pursued. Thought to be in the reserves but really on a special covert mission for the army pretending to be a translator at DTI, Sam's life was in danger from the start. Now that the mission failed and the cargo has disappeared, the army claims that he is dead and is treating his death as KIA, not MIA. Things start to unravel for him as he tries to make his way back to the states and Tyler. When the army changes its story about how he was killed—from being shot to being blown to bits beyond recognition—both Sean and Michelle become even more suspicious and determined to learn the truth. But, Tyler is persistent and so are Sean and Michelle, who seem to have been placed on the radar of HLS, DOD, and many other agencies that want them to stop interfering. Threats coming at them from all sides, shot at, beaten up, and told what would happen if they did not stand down, Sean and Michelle refuse to give up, and want the same answers that Tyler deserves.

Before he disappeared Sam Wingo brought back a young girl named Jean claiming she was his wife. Not allowing Tyler to come to the wedding, or even have knowledge of the marriage, until Sam brought her home makes the events that follow even more suspicious. We get to briefly know her, realize something is off, and wonder just who is controlling her strings. When you realize her fate and the end result you wonder what the real motive behind her being there is, and why did she suddenly disappear? Why? Secrets, betrayals, lies, deceits, and government cover-ups are just some of the themes incorporated in this complex plot.

Alan Grant has his own mission in mind, and making sure that Sam Wingo is eliminated is definitely part of his agenda. Jean Wingo's disappearance and final demise has yet to be uncovered; just what his plan is, why he needs some heavy artillery, a radio station, and weapons remain to be revealed as his vendetta stems back to the death of his parents. As the government, the president, FBI, DIA and other agencies seem more interested in Sean and Michelle then finding Sam Wingo, all roads converge as we learn that over one billion in Euros disappeared. A group of Westerners with U.S. creds flew to Afghanistan on the day before this money was supposed to be delivered to a group of Muslims, who wound up dead, hijacked

and killed, Sam losing the money and taking the fall for a mission that went south.

One sixteen year old teen just wants to clear his father's name; the FBI, DHS, and more are trying to sort it out but are using him to get to Sam. A special agent named McKinney appears to want to work with Sean and Michelle. There are leaks within the government, someone placing information in the right hands making sure things ignite. As the power goes to the top, just who is pulling all of the strings remains to be revealed.

Author David Baldacci takes readers inside a mission so covert, so undefined that many pieces and elements have not been completed, the investigation continuing as more avenues are explored and one man is investigated, his involvement apparent and his past revealed. What part does Alan Grant and why does he need a satellite? Why does he need a radio station and why the heavy artillery? What happens when they learn more about Alan Grant? What about his and others' connections with the Pentagon? Just who is providing him with the information he needs, and who is the leak?

As the pieces of the picture start to fit within the frame the fragile edges begin to come apart as Sean and Michelle face more than just the FBI and Homeland Security, but the president of the United States too. Learning more about Grant, why he was so hateful and what his plans were will give help readers understand the extent someone will go to justify his revenge. A president whose actions might cost him his life and whose policies revert back to Grant's father's involvement during the Iran-Contra scandal during the Reagan administration. *Iran-contra affair, in U.S. history, secret arrangement in the 1980s to provide funds to the Nicaraguan contra rebels from profits gained by selling arms to Iran. The Iran-contra affair was the product of two separate initiatives during the administration of President Ronald Reagan. The first was a commitment to aid the contras who were conduct-*

ing a guerrilla war against the Sandinistan government of Nicaragua. The second was to placate "moderates" within the Iranian government in order to secure the release of American hostages held by pro-Iranian groups in Lebanon and to influence Iranian foreign policy in a pro-Western direction.

When Tyler receives a strange message from Kathy he rushes to meet her only to be foiled by someone claiming to be a special agent. Kathy and Tyler face the kidnappers, hoping to stay alive until someone can rescue them. But, the kidnapper is clever until the tables are turned on him. With so many players it is hard to tell just who the next victim will be as one clever and diabolical killer justifies his actions within his own mind, and does not care about the consequences or those caught in his wake as this plot takes fold with a prime target you just won't believe. When the truth behind the mission comes up, who will remain standing and who will find themselves more than just a victim? Enlisting the help of his ex-wife Dana, Sean learns some vital information that might help him find Wingo and understand the mission. But, as his instructions to Dana were given, the end result could be fatal as she walks into a deadly trap. Will she survive, and who wanted her eliminated and why? Cover-ups, media leaks, blogs that go viral, articles planted to gain notoriety and to flare up the situation…this is one storyline with so many layers that it will keep you glued to the printed page from start to finish as the final chapters explode and the dramatic conclusion draws near.

When the president's voice is heard, Michelle and Sean are stonewalled and the leaks are getting bigger as information filters out from many sources and no one knows whom to trust. Greed, hate, deceit, power, and a plan that would bring the government down, embarrass the president and one man who was supposed to take the fall for it all, Sam Wingo fights not just for Tyler's life but to regain his own. What happens when the president wants them to stand down? Who is controlling the events and who wants Sam out of the way and why?

How many lives will end and how many will be destroyed as Sean and Michelle and the best intelligence analyst named Edgar Roy work together, hack into computers, systems, files, and governments to bring down a conspiracy that goes so far up that the end might just bring our government down. Once again author David Baldacci brings Sean and Michelle into explosive situations and near death experiences, and provides a surprise ending that only he can deliver. What is next for our ex-secret service agents? Were they able to save Tyler and Kathy? Who was behind this plot from the beginning and set up Sam Wingo? What's next for them, and will the author bring Sam back to work with them again? What about Dana? Will she come between Sean and Michelle? Only author David Baldacci knows the answer to these questions as King and Maxwell provide the suspenseful, fast paced action in this outstanding novel.

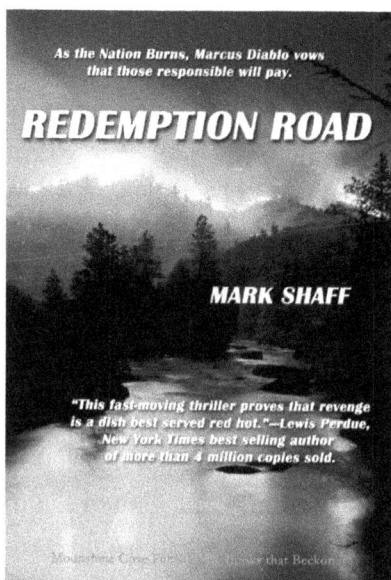

REDEMPTION ROAD
Mark Shaff
Page Count: 244 pages
ISBN: 978-1937327217
Formats: paperback, eBook

Star rating: ★ ★ ★ ★ ★

REVIEW BY FRAN LEWIS

Two young boys find themselves alone, struggling for survival while their father frantically searches for their mother. A simple camping trip turns into a nightmare for one family when the two boys and their father return from fishing and behold a scene right out of a horror movie. Watching their personal belongings being torn apart, rifled through, and destroyed, they stand helplessly apart from the scene not wanting the intruders to realize they are being watched. Mark Diablo refuses to buckle under when realizing Anne is gone, his need to find her more than just vital.

Who would take this woman and why? Where was she and how would he begin to search were questions that would have to wait until his two sons were safe. Explaining the plan, because he always had one when things went wrong, the two boys realize that they will have to be quite grown up, do what is asked of them, and create the necessary diversion needed for their father to succeed in finding their mother.

Events change; Mark sees Anne and realizes that he can do nothing to rescue her. Able to get in contact with his son, his friends at their lodge, and the sheriff, things start to fall into place, but just how remains to be seen. Questions asked, the boys and Marcus record their remem-

brances on paper, and then the FBI arrives and the tenure and tone of the investigation takes on a more sterile and stark atmosphere. Bodie and Garrett do their best to not show that they are afraid as they are taught to withstand a lot, hold their own, and man up you might say. As the author switches gears we learn more about Annie, her fate, and why she was taken. But, even with her will to survive and the fact that she is trying to hold it together, will it be enough?

Next we meet Ricky, the man who ordered her taken, who is behind what is about to happen, and from what one of the men who got caught stated has orchestrated something so horrific that this terrorist attack, which this is, will horrify and light up the world in quite a different way. When Marcus captures two of the men, kills one, and tortures the other, what he learns is just the tip of the iceberg, and what he recovers has yet to be revealed. Five cell phones, or something that looks like a phone, are recovered, but he only turns in four to the sheriff, holding onto one battery in order to learn just what this is, how it can cause fires, and what the end result might be. Hearing Ricky's voice, his father's, and then how he became involved is quite chilling.

Within Annie there is strength, determination, and the hope that she will survive. On

Marcus's birthday a startling message is received, and on hers one that is quite different. As the FBI fail in their attempt to find her and bring her home alive, the rage in Marcus fills after hearing her words and seeing the result. Deciding that revenge is going to be the answer and finding that in what he had taken from the other two terrorists the link to those in charge was found, what Marcus decides to do will make the reader question the wisdom of his decision.

Throughout the entire ordeal his family and his mother hold fast and long to support him every step of the way. His son, Garrett, has a psychic connection with Annie that allows him to convey her words, which he hears during his dreams, to the family. But, the finality of it all and the end result will burn throughout Marcus more than the raging infernos that these terrorists have set all over the forest areas in the United States.

After convincing Agent Reynolds of the FBI that he needs to step up and consider what he wants, the result will bring his children and his brother's family to Australia and relative safety. Finding one of the terrorists vitalizes Marcus; what he does to him and his treatment of this person is graphically depicted in such detail and the descriptions so sharp and clear that you might feel part of the scene yourself. Learning what he does reveals something that might send more than chills down the reader's spine as we learn about a sleeper cell in the United States. Imagine all of these terrorists working right next to any one of us, living next door and planning to destroy our country after reaping the benefits of our services, economic advantages, and medical services. Imagine creating a virus so deadly and a vehicle to ignite such horrific fires that millions if not billions of dollars will have to be spent to restore the lands and forests destroyed, the water system that was contaminated, and fund and create the medicines needed to save those that are so ill. But, Marcus does not stop at this man...he decides to go after those who implemented and orchestrated this plot. What he does will allow the reader to ask this question: Right or Wrong? Would you go to the same lengths to avenge the death of someone you truly loved as he did Annie? Would you be ready to risk it all? Think about what he does and how he carries out his plot, and ask yourself: What would you do?

Marcus is more than just resourceful as we learn about a covert group called Force 10, meet them and understand their goals. Hoping to become part of their group, enlist their help to take down those that killed Annie, we meet Colonel Sam Webb, a young tech genius named Jamie, and another named Liam, expert in arms and explosives. But, it would take much more to pull off what he had in mind. Imagine being able to steal billions if not trillions from the one man who started this all? As Marcus becomes part of this group the author shares the intense physical and mental training required and introduces him to someone that might play more than just a role as doctor in his life.

The vehicle they had to board the Takbir...the method and how they managed to do it will astound the reader. Take the journey with Force 10—Marcus and his brother Glen, a financial genius—and enter the world of terrorists, Jihads, and find out what happens when one man will do anything, including risk serious harm and pain, to avenge the death of someone so precious as his wife Annie. But, the story takes a different turn when those in charge test Marcus before being allowed to present his plan and become part of the group. Along with his son, Garrett, he now has a connection to Annie and is able to communicate with her, see her as a ghostly vision and listen to her words. Annie knows what he has endured and what he will endure, and with the help of his younger son he learns even more. Will it be an eye for an eye or a death for a death? Will he kill Adad? What will the final outcome be? Some endings are predictable. Some leave you wondering what is next, as this one does. Marcus Diablo: One man determined to find redemption:

the act of atoning for a mistake or particular fault. Is Marcus hoping to redeem himself for the guilt he feels for not insisting that Annie accompany them fishing? Would she have been taken anyway? The ending will give you much pause for thought. The final outcome for those that were behind the attack you will have to learn for yourself. Is this over or has it just begun? You won't know until the author releases: *Saint or Sinner: The Next Marcus Diablo Adventure.*

In the words of his son Bodie, "Make sure you survey the slope. Spot the potential danger zones, plan your exit route, and if the whole mountain starts to come down…." The rest you will have to learn but one plan you need to make right away is to read this exciting, fast paced novel filled with tons of technological research, information and much more.

Let's give this book: FIVE WONDERFUL DREAMS

Mark Rubinstein talks with Mark Shaff regarding *Redemption*

Why did you write a novel?

That's the million-dollar question. The easy answer is because I've always wanted to. The more complicated answer is I wanted to see if I had the imagination, talent, and perseverance to be a viable commercial fiction writer.

Did you always want to be a writer?

I have been writing for a long time, but as far as writing a novel it was an idea that I've had in the back of my mind. So when the economy took a digger, I found myself with time on my hands and this idea for a story and once got started it sort took on a life of its own.

Where did the idea for the book come from?

A few summers back I was at a barbeque, and I overheard a snippet of conversation a group of men were having about all the fires that were burning in the west. At the time there was over a million acres burning in Nevada, northern California, Colorado, New Mexico, and other intermountain western states. Anyway these guys were talking about the devastation these fires were wrecking and one of the men said,

"It's terrorists." And from those two words a light bulb went off in my head and the story was born.

A first time novelist, do you have a writing or literary background?

No. My only credit as a writer is that I am a voracious reader. I, like many avid readers, I suppose, have finished many a book only to put it down and say, "I can write that."

In terms of characters how did you go about developing them?

In truth, I wrote what I know, and what I mean is that I developed characters from life experience, people I've met, movies I've seen and books I've read. But mostly I bastardized many of the people I know very well, like family: brothers, sisters, and close friends. I took physical and personality characteristics and mashed them up and to use a term of the current generation, re-mixed them like dub-step.

The book has a broad geographical sweep, how did you decide on that and have you been to all the places you wrote about?

The geographical movement of the book was part conscious decision and part evolution. There are many places I used as scene setting that I have visited; there are also some I have not. This is perhaps one of the great things about writing in this age of information, in that there are mountains of descriptive and detailed information available on virtually any place in the world. I'm not talking about textbook information, facts and statistics, although that information is available and important, I'm talking about personal, first-hand accounts of what an area, or region looks, smells and feels like, what the people are like, how they live, the hardships they must endure. So with a good imagination, and I have that, a writer can create descriptive scenes that capture the essence of a location even though they may not have ever been there.

Do you see any other applications for this novel, for example could you envision it as a movie?

Oh yeah. But then again I can't imagine any writer of a commercial work of fiction who couldn't see their work adapted to the big screen. That would be like the grand slam of writing to get your novel picked up to be a movie. How great would that be?

So if it was to be a film, who would you see playing the primary roles?

Its funny you ask. While I was writing the many drafts, we would play this game, my wife and sons and I. The lead role of the Marcus Diablo character was unanimously Mark Walberg. I'm sure there are others but for us he has the look, age, and attitude to portray Marcus, at least as I imagine him. The other roles are more flexible, although I really like Ed Harris as Colonel Sam Webb. Like Mark Walberg, he has the right look, is the right age, and he does a great refined southern accent.

What is the thing you like most about writing?

The solitary nature of creating a story it's just you and the words.

What is the thing you like least?

The business. In retrospect, the writing was the easy part; this, the marketing and promoting, is the hard part. Don't get me wrong, I love talking about the book…it is the getting to the point where that is even a possibility that's a pain. Not to mention that the industry as a whole stands behind this impregnable wall and operates on the "don't call us, we'll call you," business model. Which, by the way, doesn't work in any business I have ever owned, or been affiliated with, over the last thirty years.

What are you working on now?

I have another book with Marcus Diablo and the same cast of characters. It's a good story and I left so much undeveloped in the first book that there is a lot to work with. I'm excited about it and hope to have it ready sometime the winter of 2014. I'm also working on two other projects that are entirely different.

As a first time novelist, what is the one thing that you learned that might benefit other first time writers?

Let go of your work. For me, I was so attached to the manuscript, to the characters, it was like I was the story, I was the characters. But it became clear that if I wanted to get a publishing deal, and have a chance of making this project successful, I was going to have to distance myself from my writing. The reality is, if you are fortunate enough to get an agent or a publisher, and then sell your work, you do just that, you sell it. It no longer belongs to you and changes can be made with or without you. The bottom line is you must be willing to make changes and you must listen to other professionals, like a good editor. There are people out there whose job it is to critique your work; the reality is as a writer you don't need to know what's right about your work, you need to know what's wrong, and this has to come from someone more objective than the writer himself.

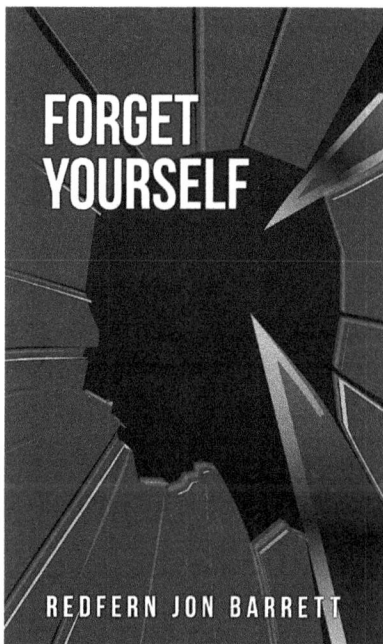

FORGET YOURSELF
Redfern Jon Barrett
Page Count: 244 pages
ISBN: 978-1484929131
Formats: paperback, eBook

Star rating: ★ ★ ★ ★ ★

REVIEW BY FRAN LEWIS

A mask hides your face so that no one knows who you are and what you look like. But, what about hiding your past and plotting it out so that you have absolutely no memories of your life, who you are, your name or where you came from? Take a magic slate and create a picture or a simple design. With a flick of a wrist or just pulling the top of the slate, the entire picture disappears as if it were never there.

What would you do if your past was erased and you lived without an identity in a world that is defined by the four walls within your confined living space, or within a community that has been created within its own caste system? What would you do if you wound up somewhere with other adults, devoid of their identity, confused and afraid?

The place these people are confined to is referred to as The Collective and their names are based on a physical attribute that is indicative to that person. We meet and hear from Blondee, named because of her hair color. Others are named because of something written on their clothing, or an attribute that might describe them. Each person within this world is there because they have committed some type of crime. Those with low-level crimes are separated from those who have committed moderate to more serious crimes. Each newcomer is placed and sentenced based on some type of sense of what they did or someone's intuition. Crimes against property, sexual, robbery, and others are classified according to their severity.

Within this story each character has a book where they write down things they remember. It could be something dealing with the weather, an animal, or even a moment that comes to mind. These memories are placed in their book as if they are creating their own chapters and will be able to recreate what has been erased from their mind. Rules are made, but who makes them? This is a community of people whose minds are as fragile and delicate as eggshells. Who could crack in seconds if not careful?

When we meet Blondee we learn about her relationship with someone named Keradine and someone named Tie. Although these relationships are rather strange, they help the reader get to understand her and know more about what her mind and thoughts are like from the little she reveals. Three men and a woman make up where she lives with all of their memories gone. However, for some innate reason, all know how to care for themselves and understand their basic wants and needs, yet have no idea why.

As Blondee shares things she remembers like food, earthquakes, or even the animals she remembers, she records this in her book in order to remember and hopefully build it. How do you establish law in an environment that is so chaotic and disorganized? What they all know and record is that they are all there because they committed a crime. Her fingers are long so she is deemed or labeled a thief. No one really remembers their crime or even committing one, so how did someone or something put them where they are?

Hearing Blondee as she receives her rations, we understand that one person controls the book, doles out the rations, and decides on what they are allowed to choose to eat and if they are entitled to anything else. Living in a triangle or hut, she has to find her own way. Finding friendship with two others and sharing the book does help her to start remembering places, objects, and things that can be added within the confines of the pages of the book.

When Blondee's memory is triggered and she realizes she sees a vision within the opening of her hut that of a woman made of stone chasing dogs and other animals. The after-mist and the stench of decay that follows remind her of death, but she has no idea why. From this experience and having possession of the book we learn more about what has been inscribed by others when they write about songs, music, recipes and the meanings of things that they might have known but have no idea why.

In a world that has been created for them, and their penance being administered by others who decide how they live and what they eat, this world is filled with prisoners who are trying to break free. Blondee lives within her own world desiring to be alone, not take on a mate at this point, and leaving what some would say is the security of her assigned area to find out more about those who are distances away.

What will she learn about the Moderates and those that have been labeled violent? Is this real or is this something that someone is writing in this book and making it happen? Water and food just appear! People decide on their lifestyle and yet their minds are clear; their thoughts make sense, but nothing else does. How do you live in a world that has no past and is creating its own present? Remembering and sharing your thoughts would be more meaningful if you had someone to share them with. When isolated and all alone with what you are creating and your memories, what kind of life is that? Will Blondee remember her first days there and those that she met? Will she begin new relationships, or pretend to talk to those not really there? Could these people have been drugged, brainwashed, or be part of some kind of mind control game that presented them with no memories and erased who they were? What happens when your every thought becomes what is placed between the pages of a book, where memories flood into different minds and are shared within its pages? Whose life is it anyway?

Within the next two books we learn about Frederick; we hear his voice, visit the Moderates, and learn about her relationship with Burberry and her love for both her and Frederick. In this world the people that are living there exhibit the same grievances, problems, and flaws that we do in our world today. From drinking to gambling to trying to remember their pasts each step of the way, adding to the book and then forgetting.

As Blondee becomes more comfortable in her own skin and life we learn of the many changes in their community, how the rations change, the losses and the gains, and we begin to see a different side of society. But, there is more for her and the others to inscribe in the book as you read it long with those living there you realize that each entry relates to something each one of us should remember: Don't pry into the lives of others. After a loss: Come back to yourself. There are many important entries that will make readers stop, think and pause for thought as you begin to wonder whether the author is trying to tell you, the reader, to embrace who you are, remember to appreciate those you love, and understand it could vanish in a split second.

Within the story we hear many voices, and Blondee presents several not really knowing which one she really is, which world she is in, and why when wanting to create change for those living in this place she is shunned, criticized, and told to leave things the way the way they are. She is told that changing anything or the course of any events or writing in the book would be harmful to the others. Blondee wants more and she wants her memories back, and will do anything to regain them.

Something happens and the author reveals what is buried and uncovered, which sets off a chain of memories that flood her mind, and the result will take her into many worlds. Who is Blondee? Is she Tanned, Tie, someone's lover, wife, rich, poor, and a sister hoping to protect her brother? Who is she? That is something that you the reader will have to decide for yourself. Take the final steps and journey with her when she reveals the truth about what it means to Forget Yourself, or have your mind and memories wiped out. Why turning back is not an option, why the choices you make will affect more than just your life, and how drifting between worlds might have taught her how to survive where she winds up!

Friends can change your life. Their thoughts can affect your every move. This is a story of love, hate, greed, despair, discontent, hope, and life, finding purpose, renewal and deceit. Living in squalor, living high, living moderate: Just living! Forget Yourself: Can you really? Some would like to, but others like Blondee…will she ever remember? What happens when so many memories flood her mind,? The reader takes many journeys to many places, and meets many of her friends, lovers, and learns some of the truths behind her life. Forget Yourself: Why would you want to? Embrace who you are!

This is one novel that will make readers understand the importance of living your life as who you are. Following your own destiny and realizing that some people cannot deal with change, while others want to make this better. What will you write when it's your turn to inscribe in the book?

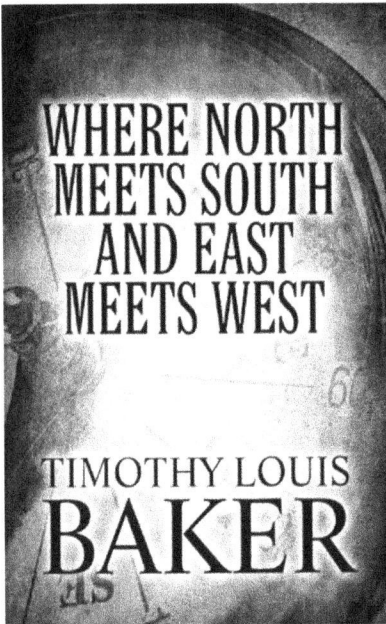

WHERE NORTH MEETS SOUTH AND EAST MEETS WEST

Author: Timothy Louis Baker
Page count: 176
ISBN: 978-1448919734
Formats: Paperback

Star rating: ★★★★★

Getting to know the author:

Growing up on a farm in rural Ohio I was sort of sheltered from the rest of the people I later became to associate with, and being an adventurous type I invented my own mischief and so began to merge with the aforementioned crowd when I became a young man. This led to a lot of getting into trouble and I drifted across North America all throughout my life, first getting into drugs with newly made friends in my hometown and then hitchhiking soon followed.

I also was nearly killed immediately following a death threat by a boy at school who was considered a black magic warlock. What first was believed by even me to be a form of punishment instilled by my criminal behavior soon turned out to be running for my life, but not from my fellow prisoners in jails, prisons, and mental institutions, but literally the law enforcement and ruffian henchmen they employed to be hit men to murder me. I often wound up on the wrong side of the bars for protection against them.

The thinking was that it was easier to stay away from anybody in there, including the cops them-selves, than it would be on the outside. There were a lot of close calls and I almost died in the jailhouse by an overdose given to me by those illegally operated syndicates of law enforcement officials.

In my 20s I lived in the mountains and backwoods of Kentucky, Minnesota, Tennessee, Arkansas, Ontario, and British Columbia. I learned to survive in the woods for four years and on the road hitchhiking for 30,000 miles, as well as twelve years of incarceration or confinement in juvenile, jails, prisons, mental institutions, and a group home.

My life has been filled with the crime of the times, but my argument is that I was innocent in that I had reason for doing what I did to save my life, and that was the only reasoning behind my criminal past. Now I live in an apartment in another Ohio town.

I haven't had any trouble with the law in ten years and don't plan on having any more of it, either, for the remainder my lifetime. Because I have cleared my name with the court system and now believe in how I live rather than run from them, I would confront my earlier enemies and fight with them in their own court system.

Interview with Timothy Louis Baker, author of Where North Meets South and East Meets West

What made you decide to share your story?

The fast and adventurous life of being into crime and drugs was interesting to me to write about in an autobiography, including the law enforcement, judicial officials, and their ruffian henchmen that were paid hit men hired to murder me but not enough by itself. I'm sure there are books like that out there, but the supernatural events including the in the flesh visit to Heaven and all the rest, gave me the story that I thought would eventually attract millions, and so I wrote my autobiographical works and some other books too.

Which parts of your autobiography were the most difficult to write about and why?

The hardest thing to write about were the parts about the syndicate of law officers especially who are supposed to save and protect life, liberty, and the pursuit of happiness, and since I had none of that, moreover they were trying to have me killed. Really such a thing is so hard to deal with anyway, but it makes me very sorry that there are men like that out there in these high positions that are so corrupt that instead of serving others serve only themselves when they can get away with it, as in my case. I find that quite disturbing and hope it is not too many more years and centuries away that this sort of thing will be a part of the past from a certain point on. It already is the most harmful part of my past of all things that have happened.

Share your relationship with your family

I have been very connected with my parents all throughout my life because I had always used my hometown for a home base until it came to be an impossibility to do so anymore.

How did working with your father keep you connected with your family?

Working for Dad on his farm was always an advantageous situation, because I could come and go not only when there was work to be done but any other time I wanted to practically. By being there on the farm working for my father there was always the contact I had with my entire family when they showed up while I was there anyway. That came in handy later when I had a son myself and was not able to take care of him because my life was still sought after. Then my ex couldn't take care of him either, found so by a court of law, so my sister that couldn't have children and wanted them took over and requested highly and mightily in that court to let her take my son in and care for him, until this day. If I had not been family oriented and my sister offering to take care of my son he may have ended up in a foster home and maybe I'd have been dead, murdered by criminals working for cops working for probation officers and a judge.

What caused you to take drugs?

I began to experiment because of peer pressure and my own personal curiosity, combined with the fact that I was just getting out there in life at that age and opportunity to get high the first time so I gladly took it. I ran with the party crowd and found that rewarding. I never knew what it would lead to but I soon found out the worst of it.

What part of your life would you change if you could and why?

I have no control over other people's actions other than to join or reject them if I choose, to walk away when possible, or to run away if necessary. However if I could change any part of my life so far would be that those lawmen and higher ups wouldn't have sought after my life. Thus the only way I know of to do this would be if I hadn't ever been in trouble with the law and they wouldn't have been after my life to murder me or have me murdered. Maybe if I had never taken that first drug, perhaps the incident of making fun of a boy at school would have passed off as a lark and incredibly nothing else would have been done. Instead I was forever later in the wrong situation that has lasted for all my life, even though that original warlock is now dead, I'm still harassed and haunted by the men that took his side, trying to make a buck and some status with their fellow syndicate members and anyone else learning of their reputation.

When creating your autobiography, how did you outline the events in order to share them with readers?

This autobiography is different with all my other books writing them start to finish without too much to add or delete or move from one place to another. I began the story of my life with writing notes on pieces of scrap paper and piling them up in no certain order upon my kitchen table. When I knew I had just about everything that would ever be of interest to a reader, except for the parts I kept secret in my head, I then got computer access and began typing them into my book's file. When I was done, since the computer was not entirely reliable and was wearing out quickly, I made a crude printout of the first draft of my book. Then I was right because the computer broke down very soon after I finished making the printout. Later I was incarcerated into jail, a mental institution, and finally restricted somewhat in a group home. There from court on the way to the group home I regained my original first draft, at which time I worked at a local business. I was allowed at the group home and earned money to buy a brand new computer. I had to type everything over again into the computer though because it was so faulty and also because it was not on disk. Then for a few years I rearranged my second manuscript, adding my own secret passages, and came

up with a compilation that with a little more work was able to produce *Where North Meets South and East Meets West* as is published by PublishAmerica presently.

Who is or was your greatest support?

Which friends were really good friends and which proved to be the opposite?

I have had friends all over the nation and some of the old timers that taught me about the mountains were the ones closest to being really good friends. Because most of the rest of the people that picked me up hitchhiking and in and out of institutions soon passed from memory, because as individuals there are just too many for me to recall them all personally. I can remember some of them but not the way you do close friends when you aren't moving all over the place all the time and they all sort of meld together so nobody gets this big portion of your attention and keeps that attention occupied for very long periods of time. I guess maybe I've met so many people that I don't even really try anymore.

If you could relive one incident what would it be and why?

Oh, that's easy, I will relive one certain incident over again…where I was in the ascension into Heaven. I will be there and live again the same thing I was doing there, making love to someone I did love, and go on from there. But that won't be until everyone and everything has taken it's own course and all life from earth is gone before it is all recreated into Heaven, where everyone and everything was young and beautiful and lived forever. That's the part that I will go back to, and actually will live over again, only next time it will be in my celestial body.

After writing your story what did you learn about yourself that you did not know before?

What I learned from it all was not only that I could be a writer and an author, but also that I had a voice and could use it in society and that people might listen. That helped a lot because in everybody's eyes so far, I was just a common criminal. Little did they know that I did what I had to do to survive at all and nobody reckoned why.

What are the many places that you traveled to and which ones stand out and why?

The North Country of Michigan, Minnesota, Ontario, and British Columbia have to be the places that I most like, and that was because of their remarkable beauty, especially the virgin portions of those territories that were so pristine and untrammeled, they must take first place in my heart, mind and soul.

Which place was the most memorable and why?

Would have to be the secluded wilderness ranch where I was allowed to stay for several weeks because it was the heart of wilderness twelve miles off the main Alaska Highway and on down a series of dirt roads. I would be all alone there for days at a time and not a soul would see me unless I wanted to be seen.

What are your other titles?

An Experience Heaven Sent; *My Life's History in Poetry*; *Fantastic Florida Fun*; *Crime and Drugs on Trip City Street*; *Wilderness Generations*; *American Lives Past*.

What are you going to write next?

I plan on writing sequels to both of my mystery thrillers *Fantastic Florida Fun* and *Crime and Drugs on Trip City Street.*

How many drafts did you go through before you decided that this title was ready to be published?

Three.

How can readers get to know you better?

I am on Facebook, Twitter, Pinterest, Goodreads, LinkedIn, LibraryThing, my websites and my publisher's websites.

Author's Links:
Website: http://fantasticfloridafun.com
Blog: http://timbaker.bookblogworld.com
Where North Meets South and East Meets West Author Enhanced Website: http://sbpra.com/authortimothybaker/
AuthorsDen: http://www.authorsden.com/timothylbaker
Books are available on Amazon, Barnes & Noble, Books*A*Million, many other online bookstores

FEATURED ROMANCE

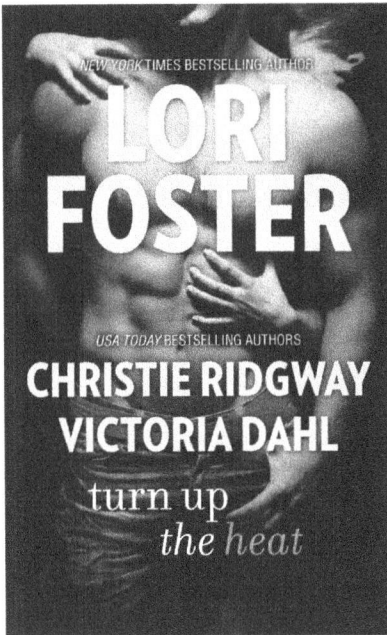

TURN UP THE HEAT
(Beach House No. 9)
Lori Foster, Christie Ridgway,
Victoria Dahl
Page Count: 336 pages
ISBN: 978-0373778386
Formats: paperback, eBook

Star rating: ★ ★ ★ ★ ★

REVIEW BY FRAN LEWIS

Brendan Carlise/Brick is one hot man. When he walks into a room he takes most women's breath away. Joining a friend at the local diner, he immediately takes a shining to the sweet, kind, and definitely breathtaking young waitress, Merrily Loveland. Oblivious to his looks, not even realizing the effect she has on him or any other man, Merrily goes about doing her job and taking great care of her customers. But, something about her drives him to want to learn more about her, and getting to know her better would offset his usual way of dealing with women and just might turn into something more.

When Merrily approaches him in the diner and brushes his shoulder with her hand, she gives him what he thinks is an opening to get closer to her. But, she has other things in mind, and when she finally corners him alone, her request of him will definitely seem out of character for her, drive him into a frenzy, and force him to confront his own true motives and feelings for her.

Getting to know her would mean passing the ultimate test:

No, it's not her parents or a child. In order for Brick to get closer to Merrily he had to pass the test of her three cats and two dogs, making sure that everyone gets along. But, Brick loves animals and does not mind helping Merrily walk and feed them. He also offers, since he runs a hardware store and his friend Jesse is a carpenter, to build her a doggie door so her pets can go out into the yard to get fresh air and are safe.

But, things get a little heated when another person becomes involved. Her landlord and neighbor, Tonya, although a good friend, gives Merrily pause for thought when inviting her over to discuss the door and other repairs that need to be done, feeling insecure in her presence. Both Brick and Merrily have a hard time resisting each other and she has no clue about how he really feels about her. But, presenting him with an offer he cannot and will not turn down creates some hot and steamy moments, tension between the two of them, and this no-commitment deal just might surprise them both and hopefully allow them to both eventually come up for air.

Turn Up the Heat sets the tone for the next two stories to follow. The air is really sizzling, the fire is turned up, and Brick and Merrily have to decide just where this is going. When the truth about her and her past comes out and someone from it shows up, what will the result be? Will Merrily decide to return to someone that really didn't appreciate who and what she is, or will she take what is right in front of her and finally realize that she might have found more than just Mr. Right? As the tension heats up and she finds herself making excuses, a friend's comment might turn the tide. Will she and Brick decide to up their game and relationship? You will have to read *Love Won't Wait* by author Lori Foster to find out. With characters that are vividly described and scenes that are tastefully yet graphically depicted, this is one short novella you will enjoy reading on a cool summer's night or to warm you up and turn up your own heat in the cold winter.

Turn up the Heat: Three novellas all intertwined in the sense that all three men are determined to change the mind sets of all three women that they care about: Merrily, Meg, and Eve tempt and taunt Brick, Caleb, and Brian with their offers that cannot be refused. Each one wondering if a real relationship is possible, and three men that will teach these women that love might win out!

Interview with romance author Lori Foster

AUTHOR BIO

Since first publishing in January 1996, Lori Foster has become a *Waldenbooks*, *Borders*, *USA Today*, *Publisher's Weekly* and *New York Times* bestselling author. Lori has published through a variety of houses, including Kensington, St. Martin's, Harlequin, Silhouette and Samhain. She is currently with Berkley/Jove.

Lori believes it's important to give back to the community as much as possible, and for that reason she ran special contests in conjunction with a publisher, facilitating many first sales for new authors. She routinely organizes events among authors and readers to gather donations for various organizations.

Lori hosts a very special annual "Reader & Author" event in West Chester, Ohio. Proceeds from the event have benefited many worthy causes, including the Hamilton County YWCA Battered benefited many worthy causes, including the Hamilton County YWCA Battered Women's Shelter, the Animal Adoption Foundation, The Conductive Learning Center for children with spina bifida and cerebral palsy, and The One Way Farm, Children's Home.

- 2007 —Lori put together *The Write Ingredients* a cookbook of recipes donated by popular authors. Proceeds from the cookbook go toward Lori's ongoing "Troop project" of collecting and mailing fun, and sometimes necessary, items to our troops.

- 2008 — Lori coordinated with other authors of her choosing, and through Berkley, arranged for the publication of *The Power of Love*, a special romance anthology of novellas about empowering women. All author and agent proceeds from the anthology go to the Hamilton Co YWCA Battered women's shelter.

- 2009 — *Tails of Love*, another romance anthology with Lori and other contributing authors, was published through Berkley with all agent and author proceeds to benefit The Animal Adoption Foundation.

- 2010 — *The Gift of Love* romance anthology, with Lori and other contributing authors, was published with proceeds to benefit The Conductive Learning Center, a school for children with cerebral palsy and spina bifida.

- 2011 — *The Promise of Love*, a romance anthology with Lori and other contributing authors, will be published with proceeds to benefit the One Way Farm, a home for abused and abandoned children.

- 2012 — *Love Bites*, a romance anthology with Lori and other contributing authors, was published with all agent and author proceeds to benefit The Animal Adoption Foundation.

- 2013 — *Animal Attraction*, a romance anthology that included a novella featuring Lori's popular Buckhorn Brother characters, was published with all agent and author proceeds going to benefit The Animal Adoption Foundation.

Lori has received many prestigious awards, including:

- *Romantic Times* Career Achievement Award for: Series Romantic Fantasy Contemporary Romance

- Waldenbooks: *Say No To Joe* — second "Bestselling Original Contemporary"

- Borders Group Inc.: *The Secret Life of Bryan* — "Bestselling Original Contemporary" romance title: *Jude's Law* — "Bestselling Romantic Comedy" romance title: *Back in Black* – "Bestselling Romantic Suspense" romance title

Lori Foster has been both a clue in the *New York Times* crossword puzzle and the *USA Today* Quick Cross puzzle and she enjoys visiting with readers on her Facebook Fan page, Twitter, Goodreads, and Pinterest.

THE INTERVIEW

Give our readers a brief history about your goals as a writer and author.

My goals have always remained the same—with every book I hope to be a better author with a wider audience filled with happier readers. :-)

When creating several books in a series how do you decide how many books will be within that series? Do you have several recurring characters within each series in order to ignite and spark continued reader interest? Do you include new characters in each novel?

I never, ever know upfront how many books will be in a series because I rarely know who the main characters will be in each book until they show up on the page and demand a book. Some characters remain secondary, some jump up and become a hero or heroine. I'm always as surprised as everyone else. :-)

While previous characters sometimes show up in subsequent books, each book has a new set of main characters, and each book can stand alone.

What is your first series and who are the main characters? Have you continued with this character in another series or does each series have its own protagonist?

My first series was with the Winston brothers—originally each brother appeared in an anthology. Cole, Chase, Mack...and then Zane got a single title. In that book, their cousin Joe showed up, and he eventually got his own book and expanded the series from *The Winston Brothers* to *Visitation*.

The only time I've continued with a single character was in writing as L.L. Foster with my "darker" urban fantasy series.

When creating your main characters do you often create an antagonist to spice up the plot?

You know, I don't feel like *I* create anything. The characters dictate all of it, so if they "tell me" there's an antagonist, then there is. Basically I sit down and start writing a single scene and the main characters lead me along from there, telling me the story as I type.

I read and reviewed A Perfect Storm. The characters are distinct and have a great chemistry from the start: Arizona Storm and Spencer Lark are the two main characters in this novel: What do they do and why did you pair them?

Arizona showed up in a previous novel and sort of won me over. Little by little—before I ever got to her book—she told me her secrets and demanded I tell her story. Spencer just sort of popped up one day while I was writing, and he just happened to pop up next to Arizona, and the sparks flew...it's very weird how it works for me. I literally get as surprised as the reader by what happens. :-)

This novel might be classified as romance but it has a touch of mystery and suspense too: How did you manage to blend the two genres and keep the romantic element alive?

I've been labeled Romantic Suspense, Romantic Comedy, Romantic Action & Adventure...basically, I'm all about the romance. That's the part that fascinates me. So no matter what else happens in the story, whether it makes you laugh or cry, if it's action packed or full of suspense, you are guaranteed that two people will overcome obstacles and fall in madly in love—and have some very hot sex along the way. :-)

Love Bites is another novel that I reviewed. It is a collection of five stories the following authors: Lori Foster, Catherine Mann, Brenda Jackson, Jules Bennett, and Virna DePaul: why did you decide to create this book of great stories and where do the proceeds go?

It's become a favorite pet project of mine, organizing books & stories and donating all the proceeds to one of my favorite charities.

The way the stories are published has varied over the years—from print to eBook, from many authors to just me—but the point is always to give the gift that keeps on giving. I've yet to have a book stop producing. By donating a book to a favorite charity, they will continue to get royalties for as long as the book sells.

Your new series begins with *Delicious, Men of Courage, Hot In Here* and *Getting Rowdy,* which are several of your new releases: Some you author alone and other with several other romance novelists: Tell us about the books?

Well first, those books aren't together as a series. *Delicious* is a reissue of my novella in *Star Quality.*

Men Of Courage is a reissue of an earlier anthology by the same name but with a new cover.

Hot In Here is a reissue of three older novellas grouped together under one cover. Included are *Uncovered, Tailspin,* and *An Honorable Man.*

Getting Rowdy is book #3 of my *Love Undercover* series that started with *Run the Risk* and then *Bare It All.* The #4 book in the series will be Dash Of Peril due out April 2014.

In the *Love Undercover* series, readers also meet Cannon Colter, and his book will be out Sept 2014, titled *No Limits,* and will be the 1st book in a new series.

Finally, where can everyone learn more about you, your books and your events?

The go to place for my book news is my website, www.LoriFoster.com. There, readers can see a "Connect Book List," which shows all the books connected in a series. Each book always stands alone, but it makes it easier for readers to know who the friends are.

I'm also on Facebook and have a lot of giveaways. I reply to all emails. My contact info is on my site. I also list Facebook, Twitter, Goodreads. Pinterest and PushPagein links in my email signature. Be sure to sign up for my newsletter!

BEACH HOUSE BEGINNINGS

(Beach House No. 9) Novella

Christie Ridgway

Page Count: 66 pages

Formats: eBook, audio

Star rating: ★ ★ ★ ★ ★

REVIEW BY FRAN LEWIS

Haunted by her past and losing someone she cared about caused Meg Alexander to leave her hometown and not want to return. With her sister out of town and at a wedding, she agrees to come back and take care of their business and hopefully have some time to herself.

Meeting one resident named Rex, who is ninety years young as the author relates, we learn that Meg would rather spend her time doing repairs to the beach houses they rent and have a lot of alone time. But not everything always goes as planned as the author allows readers some insight into her past and a young man named Peter.

It's been ten years since she returned home. Now at twenty-nine, she is filled with mixed feelings and yet something might change it. A figure appears at her door and the image reminds her of Peter. A short discussion and a definite check him out and check her out, lets readers know that the chemistry in this lab just might explode.

Caleb McCall is Peter's cousin, and when he calls Meg by another name she carefully handles it and corrects him. But, will she allow him into her life? Renting him one of the bungalows, she hands over the key to him and he leaves, only to return later asking her to help with his oven.

Sometimes the slightest thing can set off a chain of events that neither party will expect. Inviting himself to cook his already prepared dinner in her kitchen might be the way to go, or he could take her up on her offer to pay for dinner at the local restaurant? Will things heat up in Beach House No. 9, or will the cool summer air let them simmer?

Remembering the past brings back memories of just whom Caleb is and how she came to know him in the past. Talking about her losing Peter brings back painful thoughts, but the conversation continues over a great dinner he prepared.

Caleb is determined to win Meg's heart even if the memories of Peter flood into her mind. Within this short novella you meet two people whose lives intersected years before yet never realized the impact they would have on each other.

When Caleb reveals the real reason he came back to the Cove, why he needed and wanted to see Meg, will that change how she feels about commitment, and will she realize how much he cared for her back then and even more now?

Fear of what might happen if things don't work out stop Meg from truly giving her heart to anyone; a heart-shaped shard of abalone shell that shines in the sunlight will bring it all back and maybe even make her smile.

Losing Peter created a huge void in her heart, and the thought of losing anyone else or getting close to someone frightens her. So, what will she do? Because he's not giving up.

When Caleb relates something about his past and his true reasons for coming to the Cove, will she believe he cares? Remembering stories her mother told her and times she and her friends spent on the beach, will her childhood memories and memories of her past bring them together in the present? Find out if one short weekend can change the lives of two people forever.

Caleb, handsome, hot and Meg, so stunning he cannot resist her. Characters true to life and whose emotional upheavals and upsets are perfectly described, and the scenes that connect them beautifully described. *Beach House Beginnings*. There's more to learn as the author continues with a new series: *Cabin Fever*.

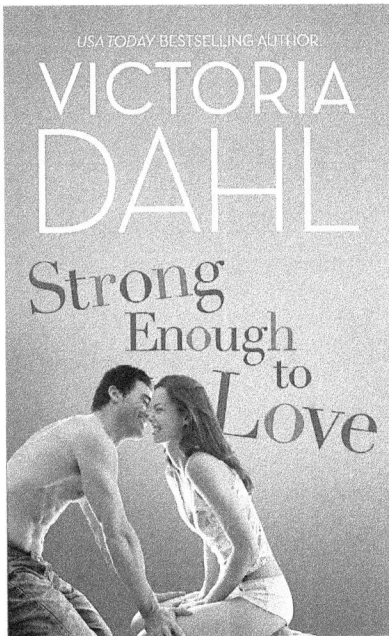

STRONG ENOUGH TTO LOVE

Novella

Victoria Dahl

Formats: eBook

Star rating: ★★★★★

When Brian Stewart left Jackson Hole, Wyoming, he left more than just a hole within the heart of photographer Eve Hill. Married to another woman and yet more than attracted to Eve, their relationship soared for a while until it didn't. Brian left wanting to give his marriage another try, leaving Eve in his wake to deal with her own feelings and fallout. Determined to find out if they could rekindle the fires that burned within them, he reenters her life but this time is determined to stay. Just seeing Brian brought back memories that infuriated Eve and emotions that were dormant, but seem to erupt like the lava in a raging volcano. But Eve, as hard as she tries, cannot ward off his advances and decides to allow him one night of passion and then move on.

Sometimes the past cannot be repaired, but the future can rebuild something better. What happens when the man you care about is off-limits and off your own radar? Do you give in to your feelings and give him a second chance, or do you walk away before you get hurt again? Eve's memories shatter her trust and the sight of Brian brings it all back. The author relates what happened between them, his decision to try again with his wife, selling Eve her gallery and then walking away. So, what happens, as Eve says, when a man, "Makes me want to give everything"? How can she forgive the fact that he walked away? Was she worth it? Why wasn't she enough reason to stay? Find out the lengths to which Brian will go to get Eve, and learn whether their relationship is *Strong Enough to Love* and last. Forgiveness, understanding, regrets and new beginnings: Will Brian and Eve get theirs?

Turn up the Heat! These three novellas all intertwined in the sense that all three men are determined to change the mind sets of all three women that they care about: Merrily, Meg and Eve tempt and taunt Brick, Caleb, and Brian with their offers that cannot be refused. Each one wondering if a real relationship is possible and three men that will teach these women that love might win out!

REVIEW BY FRAN LEWIS

EREADERS OR A 'REAL' BOOK

Mark Rubenstein

People have passionate feelings about using an e-reader or a "real" book. The arguments rage back and forth as the advantages and disadvantages of each method of reading become tired mantras promulgated by each side.

For those who favor paper books, there's the feel and smell of paper; the pleasure of having and holding a "real" book in one's hands; of turning pages; of being able to return to an earlier page; of seeing page numbers; of writing marginalia; of dog-earing a page; of seeing the cover design and the author's picture. And, there's the exquisite look of multiple bookshelves, densely packed with treasured volumes, forming a veritable history of the reader's past excursions. For some, it's a lifetime habit, a collector's paradise—a pleasure of immense proportions—one they refuse to renounce in the face of our increasingly digitized and impersonal world.

Those praising electronic books marvel at their accessibility: how easy it is to download one from the Internet, and how inexpensive it can be. Books published before 1923 are free for the downloading, encompassing virtually all classics. Those that are contemporary are deeply discounted. One can carry 1,500 or more books in a small, portable device. They love how the "cloud" holds thousands more books, obviating the need to find more shelf space. They talk glowingly of their reading devices being so light, portable, and versatile. They marvel how the font size can be changed; for how one can highlight words or paragraphs; and how by merely holding a finger over a word, obtain its definition. And of course, no paper means saving trees.

There are obvious advantages to each way of reading.

So, what's my opinion?

Simply put, I love books, whether paper or electronic versions. I'll read on whatever is available. I love being transported to another world—one beyond my own; to share the domain a writer has created. It's a fantastical realm to which I bring my own thoughts, feelings, fantasies and experiences.

And that's my point: the *experience* of taking in the writer's creation counts, not the *medium* by which it's delivered. For me, whether a book is on a device or on paper is irrelevant. So long as the writer's words are taken in by my eyes, processed by my mind, and fed into my willingness to share the writer's storytelling, I'm happy to be reading.

For me, the medium is *not* the message.

Mark Rubinstein has coauthored five medical self-help books: *The First Encounter: The Beginnings in Psychotherapy*, *The Complete Book of Cosmetic Facial Surgery*, *New Choices: the Latest Options in Treating Breast Cancer*, *Heartplan: A Complete Program for Total Fitness of Heart & Mind*, and *The Growing Years: A Guide to Your Child's Emotional Development from Birth to Adolescence*, and wrote the novels *Mad Dog House*, named a Finalist for the 2012 ForeWord Reviews Book of the Year Award (Thriller & Suspense), and *Love Gone Mad*. www.MarkRubinstein-Author.com

DIGITAL OR PRINT FOR YOUR BOOK?

Donald Riggio

How many times have you heard it said: I prefer the feel and smell of a book in my hands, something I can clutch warmly like a treasured friend?

I know I've said it, though perhaps not as romantically, but it was my assertion for a long time that I did NOT embrace the world of digital publishing and e-books. All that changed with the publication of my first novel, *Seven-Inch Vinyl: A Rock and Roll Novel*, in 2011.

Hoping to have my work published in a traditional manner, I shopped the manuscript around to a great many agents with no luck in gaining representation. My next step was to comparison shop the various "print-on-demand" options. When I found one that seemed reliable and affordable, I took a leap and self-published. I was very pleased with the results and soon had a warm and fuzzy print book readers could take to the beach or curl up with in front of a fire on a cold winter night.

However, the most surprising aspect of the process came when I learned that the book could be offered as an e-book download on Amazon.com for their Kindle reading device. A further leap resulted in my book becoming a #1 Kindle bestseller in the music category.

This year when it came time to publish the sequel, *Beyond Vinyl: The Rock and Roll Saga Continues*, I fine-tuned the process by using Amazon's self-publishing arm, *Createspace*. History repeated itself and the sequel hit #1 in the Kindle music category as well.

The benefits of this and other e-book publishers are many; it eliminates the need for an agent (saving you, the author, as much as 15% in cost), if you are reasonably computer literate you can do the format-

ting yourself saving you more money. If not, most will provide the editing, formatting, design a book cover and other amenities for an additional cost.

As a member of the Amazon family, I have a slight bias. But the flexibility to set and change the price of your book, offer promotions, and take advantage of their worldwide distribution network makes Amazon the logical choice.

The digital process gives an author total control of their work, from the creative elements through publishing and marketing, making the answer to the question *Print or Digital*, a no brainer.

––––––––––

Donald Riggio was born and raised in the Bronx, New York and has had a deep and enduring love of rock and roll music since he was a boy. His love of writing is equally enduring as is illustrated in his success as a short story and technical writer over the years.

He combined his two passions with the publication of his first novel, *Seven-Inch Vinyl: A Rock and Roll Novel*, in 2011. That book became a #1 Kindle Best Seller in the music category as did the sequel, *Beyond Vinyl: The Rock and Roll Saga Continues* published in 2012.

He also hosts a hugely successful Facebook page, where he and his 3,500+ friends discuss, post pictures, rock and roll song links and information 24/7. He invites everyone to join him.

Mr. Riggio lives in Las Vegas, Nevada, where he is currently writing the third book in his trilogy, *When Gold Turns to Gray.*

GIVING UP THE CABLE

Kenneth Weene

My parents bought our first television when I was eight. I loved it. I loved it so much that I even watched test patterns. I also watched some pretty horrible programming. But things got better—much better. There were some wonderful shows like *The Outer Limits*, *The Twilight Zone*, *Your Show of Shows*, *Ed Sullivan*, and the list goes on. Some have called those years the golden age of television.

Given that early love of television, I was taken aback by the decision my wife and I made recently: to give up our cable service. I had totally surprised myself, but the decision did make sense.

It happened this way. We were in bed and looking for something to watch. Remote in hand, we started the process. There were about eighty channels to surf. *Click, click, click.* Nothing! Well, to be fair there was a *Matlock* rerun; but how many times can I watch the same reruns? And Roz was adamantly against it. Sadly, that episode of *Matlock* was the closest we came to finding a show worth its electrons.

The reasoning that night went something like this. We have Netflix. We have Hulu. We have our computers. Why do we need to spend about $100 a month for this wasteland?

The next day we began the easy process of returning cable boxes.

As I stood in line waiting to turn those boxes in, questions crossed my mind. What had happened? Where had my beloved TV land gone? Who was responsible?

Thinking back on the great years of television, those golden years, I realized that their hallmark had been risk taking. Perhaps because nobody was teaching college classes on how to do it, writers and performers were being spontaneous and creative. Perhaps because nobody was spending a fortune to hire the most famous actors and staff, shows could be given a chance, and failure was an option. Maybe there was more risk taking because there was less competition. With only a few networks, shows had a chance to get an audience and to build over time. After all, a certain portion of the audience would end up watching a new or flailing show by default simply because that channel was the one that came in best via those old rooftop antennae or the rabbit ears perched atop the console.

Today's television lacks that risk taking. Follow the formula, copy the show that is already successful, and don't risk alienating anyone have become the standards for making programming decisions.

Besides the decline in risk taking, there is another reason for television's decline—a reason I think is at the heart of our modern American zeitgeist. In those bygone days the average person did not expect to be on television. We watched and were entertained by professionals, people whom we saw as different from ourselves. We, the fast numbers of viewers, didn't have the skills, the technology, or the expectation of being on TV ourselves. That separation of the art from the general public has disappeared. Today, everybody can make a YouTube video. Today, everybody can imagine himself or herself on television. Everyone is waiting to be discovered.

Everybody expects to be a star, which brings us to popularity, the essence of stardom. But what makes somebody popular? What makes them a star? Stars are people who do something the way the average person would do that thing if the average person could do it at all. We love the person with whom we can, in our aspirations, best identify.

Stardom is different from having great talents. People with great talent are unique; often they are often not very popular—consider opera singers, Shakespearean actors, and ballet dancers. Stars get their popularity from average people identifying with them. As television developed, the average person could not imagine being on Ed Sullivan, but (s)he could imagine screwing up like Lucy. The average person may not have aspired to the comedy of Sid Caesar, but they could surely be a Ralph Cramden or an Ed Norton.

Add that notion of stardom to the availability of technology and you have modern television, which is dominated by people who appear to be like you and me doing what they do, which is misidentified as reality. People believe it is real because they can easily identify with what is going on. Sure, they would do and say the same thing if only the occasion presented itself. What is even better for the average viewer is that (s)he often gets to vote for their favorite performer, which means voting for the person who is most like they imagine themselves to be. Reality TV viewers may not bother to vote for president or Congress, but they do love to vote for the voice, the dancer, or even the chef who best reminds them of their own aspirations.

For me, the result is a wasteland. Not because I feel superior but because I feel indifferent. I don't want to be a star so I don't identify with this star-crossed reality TV industry. As a writer, my goal is to create art. I don't want to be on The Real Writers of Hoboken; I want to write books that people will want to read long after my life is over. I want to be a real talent.

Perhaps the Golden Age of Television spoiled me, but I would prefer to have written one episode of *The Outer Limits* than to have danced with the stars for an entire season.

Besides writing opinion pieces, Kenneth Weene is co-host of It Matters Radio, editor of *The Write Room Blog*, and an author of short fiction and novels. Learn more about Ken at http://www.kennethweene.com

You can find Ken's novels in print, e-format, and audio.

REALITY PROGRAMS VS. FICTION SHOWS ON TV

Trish Jackson

In recent years reality shows like American Idol, The Voice, Survivor, Amazing Race and several others have taken over the prime time spots on the major TV networks. Like all TV shows, the good ones survive and the bad ones are dropped. But why have they become so popular?

Two words: emotional engagement. This is the primary reason for the popularity of reality shows. We identify with the participants because they are real people, just like us, as opposed to actors who are playing a role. The emotion we see is real, not contrived. We choose to champion one or more of the contestants and rejoice with them at each small success, cry real tears with them at their downfall, and celebrate their triumph when they win. We strategize for them and applaud them when they do the right thing, and scold them when they don't. We vote for them and our voice counts, while more and more shows invite us, the viewers, to actively get involved using social media. What could be better for a nation of people who love their phones and computers?

It has been suggested that the reason for their popularity is that viewers have gotten lazy and no longer want to use their intelligence in the evenings after a hard day at work. Really? The shows that occupied prime time before were detective stories like *CSI*, *Criminal Minds*, and *Law and Order*; medical shows like *House*, *ER* and *Bones*; or comedies like *Two and a Half Men* or *Rules of Engagement*.

I fail to see how they challenged the mind. Their stories are not real and the emotions the actors display all come from a script.

The truth is clear. We are no longer content with sitting on the sidelines. We want to feel real emotions and we want to interact.

Trish Jackson writes emotive romantic suspense focusing on small towns, country folk and their animals. Visit her website at *www.trishjax.com*

FRAN'S PICKS OF THE MONTH

Broken Allegiance, Mark Young
Angel Killer, P.J. Nunn
The Tenth Circle, Jon Land
My Life is a Four Letter Word, Dolores DeLuce
Forget Yourself, Redfern Barrett

Only Twelve Days, Eileen Thornton
Abe Lincoln: Public Enemy No. I, Brian Anthony and Bill Walker
Lies Betrayals and Fear: Faces 3, Fran Lewis

BOOKS DEALING WITH ISSUES

SPECIAL FOCUS: PRISON FAMILIES

THE UNVARNISHED TRUTH ABOUT THE PRISON FAMILY JOURNEY

Carolyn Esparza and Phillip Don Yow Sr.
Formats: paperback
326 pages
ISBN-13: 978-1490392387

Star rating: ★★★★★

REVIEW BY FRAN LEWIS

Think about being locked in a cell with no windows for the rest of your life. Think about not having any contact with your family unless allowed by those in charge. Think about spending years or even the rest of your life deep within the walls of a prison only dealing with those that have been placed near you, with you, or next to you as company. Think about this and many other things before you commit a crime. But, not everyone that goes to prison is guilty. Some are incarcerated and even wrongly executed in order to clear the dockets and close a case.

All too often no one really looks into anything long and hard, nor do many prosecuting attorneys play by the legal rules to find out the truth. I wonder sometimes whether they look further to see if they have arrested the wrong person or stop after making an arrest. When you read what the authors of this book share with you and learn the truth about the prison system, you will shudder, shake, and definitely want to make sure that others learn the hidden truths, lies, deceits and betrayals that go unnoticed, unpunished, and discarded when lawyers and

judges do not realize that some are not guilty, some are, and the treatment received is inhumane.

Learn how to protect your loved one and yourself from having to deal with legal blunders and mistakes. Learn after reading this outstanding resource what questions you should be asking when seeking an attorney to defend you or a family member. Learn what you, if arrested, need to know, the questions you have a right to ask, and understand the journey that you will be taking, along with those that are left behind on the outside. The information is presented in a clear and concise manner and the chapters and sections are outlined to separate the information shared.

Both the emotional and legal standpoints are presented in each chapter and from the moment those handcuffs are placed on the person's wrist, blame is presented, and you learn and feel just what anyone placed behind bars will endure. What about those left behind? Should they bear any shame? How do your family members, especially young children, deal without a parent for so long? How do you make them understand that your path should not be the same one they take?

The same way you want to make sure that you get the most for your money when you are purchasing a high ticket item, you want to make sure that when you "shop" for an attorney you get the most to protect your life and you. Within pages 8-12 the authors give you explicit information that is invaluable when looking for not only a criminal defense attorney but also any lawyer in general.

Although the questions that you should ask and follow up on relate to this type of case, you can adjust many of them to fit just about any situation. For example, "Is my case in your area of expertise?" can relate to any area. "I understand you are busy, but what are your thoughts about frequent updates?" These are just two of the many questions that you need to ask when looking for someone to take your case. Followed by going to court and explaining the emotional and legal areas involved, the authors include a simple yet complex chart titled, The Sequence of Events in the Criminal Justice System. Then "The Journey Begins," with finding the attorney, your family's relationship with that attorney, and how bail is set, what you might have to give them besides money in order to insure that you meet the requirements, what you are expected to do and not do, and the Unvarnished Truths behind what really happens after you are arrested. Expect postponements, don't be surprised if the judge and the opposing counsels are friendly, do not expect your lawyer to devote all of his time to you and your case, and live with the unknowns and uncertainties for months. Another Unvarnished Truth is that bonding a loved one might or might not be in your best interest, and that the bondsman is really not there to protect your rights but their own. Read the checklist on page 21 when deciding whether to post bail or bond for a family member or even a friend. Pre-trial hearings are discussed and how they pertain to felonies is discussed on pages 23-25.

What you might find quite compelling and enlightening is the true meaning of plea bargaining, the pitfalls so many fall into when they agree to plea, and the many reasons you might want to think before agreeing. Important points brought out on pages 26-34 will give defendants pause for thought for taking this final step. Remember that if you agree to a plea you are admitting to being guilty. With few exceptions, "accepting a plea bargain agreement is final, if accepted by the judge." It does not necessarily mean that the judge will award you the lighter sentence even though you have agreed to plea bargain. Judges do not have to accept it. Remember something else that the authors will make you aware of: There is no accountability in the criminal justice system. Therefore judges are FREE to make up their own rules as the case unfolds. Bone chilling to say the least.

Next they take you through every step of the trial, including trauma and grief starting with the arrest, and the five steps that every person might experience in the grief process: Denial, Anger, Depression, Acceptance, and Bargaining. Within this section the authors describe the grief process and how each step of the way many people become stuck or glued and cannot move on with their own lives. But, a very crucial point is made about children and hiding the fighting from them, and hopefully not allowing them to hear the cruel and mean things people might be saying or are saying about their parent that is in jail.

Children are smart and they learn from adults at times, and hearing that one of their parents is lower than low and does not deserve the time of day, children are impressionable and will often live up to the same expectations of their parents and feel they are unworthy too. The frightening part is what happens when they become as the authors relate "property of the prison system," losing all contact with their family and their right to communicate with them. Then they share the fact that there is a prisoner's handbook subject to change at the whim of those in charge.

Legalities are discussed, the trial, the arrest, and the intake, and next we come to what it feels like to be a part of the system and what happens when you renter the community you lived in before. They also discuss what happens within the minds of those outside, and how some just cannot deal with the fact that a loved one is incarcerated. Denial is one way of dealing with it, and some just refuse to admit it and pretend that person is somewhere else and do not admit the truth. The authors include information about many support groups even on Facebook, and one that is quite reputable: CURE.

A recurring theme throughout is that inmates remain humans, and they remain citizens. We need to help those in prison, and also those returning to society. A special chapter on the children of prisoners brings up additional issues that many of us have not confronted. This book is loaded with information, including the Children of Prisoners Bill of Rights that I wish were the law of the land...and the federal law on filing grievances (depressing chapter).

First-hand stories of prison violence and relationships fill out the book, which concludes with useful forms that most of us would never find ourselves: power of attorney, release of information, etc. Informative, well written—you need this book. As an educator the worst you can do is stereotype family members and assume that one sibling is the same as the other. Working with students whose parents were a part of a prison family, you should never make that student feel that he/she is responsible or should feel ashamed.

The next part of the book explains visitations and the rigid and strict rules and regulations, and the difficulties faced when asking for a visit. Just hearing what the author endured, and the fact that family members undergo so many indignities and have to make sure they do not upset a guard or any other official, allows readers to understand why some decline to visit and why some prisoners have few if any visits.

The authors include the rules of what is allowed to be written, how mail, snail mail, email and other forms of communication are handled, and the types allowed or disallowed, including the rules for sending packages, books and other materials. Families have to make sure, just as the prisoners do, to follow the guidelines and the rules that can change at any moment. Author Phillip Yow shares what is allowed according to the Texas Prisoner system, and then we learn more about what happens inside and the abuse some take and refuse to report. The sad part is that so many suffer as the authors conclude with the role of many family members, defining who they are and what happens when their loved one is released.

The chapter that speaks volumes and is the most compelling is the one written by Phillip Don Yow: "Perspective From Inside Prison," will open the eyes of prison families, the public, and anyone who reads this book to the hidden truths, lies, deceits and corruption within the walls of prisons. A detailed discussion of the lack of concern for the human rights and the indignities of prisons is graphically and vividly described by the author. He relates his own experiences and how he dealt with various types of abuse as he states, "The administration could care less about what happens to inmates, and when fights or violence breaks out the guards and administration do nothing to stop it." How incidents are documented, the inept grievance process, and the many ways family members can communicate effectively with there loved one fill the pages of this compelling chapter. From financial support, to gang threats, and finally how prisoners deal with the many forms of violence and why they fear reporting it to anyone, Phillip Yow speaks out for all prisoners that have been wrongly accused and denied their basic human rights.

The most horrifying information comes in the last few pages. The author shares the fact that the basic physical comforts, necessities such as food, hygiene products, medical care, clothing that would help in the winter, safety, sense of belonging, self-esteem, respect, sense of self-actualization, and any method of bettering the prisoner making their transition back into their own community easier are denied. With no means to better themselves and little or no access to materials to help further their education, this book provides many resources for prisoners, their families, and even prison officials to open their eyes to the harsh realities that they face. Prisoners are human beings, and why they are treated as less is wrong; to me, that is *The Unvarnished Truth*!

Fran Interviews the Carolyn Esparza

If you could create a basic list or a simple handbook of the most important things that families need to address after getting that phone call, what would you include in this list? What contacts are vital? What are the most important documents needed and why?

Upon receiving a call from jail reporting your loved one has been incarcerated, despite the agonizing shock and paralyzing fear, one must quickly gather *accurate* information and certainly learn what the arrested party has to say about the arrest charges being brought against them.

Because communication with the prisoner becomes almost non-existent when jailed, you might contact the jail's booking desk to learn the reported charges against your loved one, and also ask about the first opportunity to visit the prisoner in person. In some jails, prisoners will be able to call home collect, if the family has a landline. In any case, the family must ask the prisoner their own explanation of what the charges are and exactly what happened.

The *last* thing a person should do is fork out any money on behalf of their loved one *until they have all of the relevant information*. That means *no* bond (many first-time offenders will be released on their own recognizance and money is not required) and *no* attorney until *after* knowing the charges and what the prisoner has to say about their charges.

That's easier said than done, and most people won't even believe that until it's too late and they've wasted and even gone into debt by thousands of dollars due to their anxiety—they just have to get that person out of jail at all costs!

If children have been left behind with no caregiver and risk being placed in foster care, family members should quickly obtain a signed and notarized Power of Attorney (POA) from the child's incarcerated parent to be able to act on behalf of the child. Type one up (we have a copy of a POA in the back of The Unvarnished Truth about the Prison Family Journey, just for this purpose). Take it to the jail and ask to have your loved one sign it before a notary. There is a notary at the jail.

Other than the POA, only documents related to the charges against the prisoner would be needed at this point, so it's a good idea to start gathering any evidence that would help the prisoner when going to court.

This was the case with my own mother, who at age sixty, was falsely arrested for a bad check; my father immediately retrieved the receipt indicating the bad check had long ago been paid in full with cash. Unfortunately, that didn't stop the sheriff's officers from handcuffing her in front of customers, transporting her, and booking her into the county jail, where she was traumatically strip searched...but it did motivate the attorneys my parents hired to pursue the case vigorously, for a contingency fee! That one little receipt was the winning ticket when my mother sued the county, the jail, the sheriff, and the company that failed to correctly document that the bad check had immediately been paid in full in cash, for her false arrest!

Explain the initial reaction of family members and why they need to stay clearheaded? What are the rights of the defendant in court, and how can they verbalize their feelings in court if they feel they are not being treated fairly?

Initially family members will be thrust into disbelief and denial, shock and paralyzing fear. However, if they don't quickly recover, they risk being taken to the cleaners by the legal system and convicted and harshly sentenced, whether deserved or not! They MUST take some deep breaths, calm themselves enough to ask questions, and gather information, as well as make critical decisions.

Three (3) primary constitutional rights have been designated for defendants in court:

- 5th Amendment Constitutional Right against Self Incrimination

- 6th Amendment Constitutional Right to Trial by an Impartial Jury and Effective Assistance of Counsel

- 14th Amendment Constitutional Right to Due Process and Equal Protection Under the Law (Evidence of the importance of paying attention in government class!)

If a defendant believes their rights are being violated during any of the court proceedings, they have the right to speak up—even if it means interrupting the proceedings—to make mention of this fact *on the court record*, and this includes the right to *fire their attorney on the court record.*

What most people fail to realize is that even if the judge tells the defendant to "Be Quiet" and/or disallows the firing of a defense attorney (which often happens) at least the defendant has assured the issue is documented on the court record. This can be used in appealing their case if they are unjustly convicted and/or too severely sentenced. The point is to create a paper trail by getting the issue in the court record.

What are the major attributes of a good attorney? When should the defendant or family hire one?

Because the average citizen is not versed in the law, it is almost impossible to proceed with a legal matter (criminal or civil) without legal representation. So, of course an attorney is needed. However, because attorneys charge by the minute (literally) it is best to gather as much information about the case as is possible before approaching attorneys.

It is extremely difficult to pinpoint "characteristics of a good attorney," because at the outset they all "sound good." Therefore, it's much easier and even more effective to know the signs of a BAD attorney and then to react accordingly when these signs surface.

There is a good deal of information in the book *The Unvarnished Truth about the Prison Family Journey* about shopping for an attorney—questions to ask when interviewing attorneys to represent you or your loved one. The most ethical attorneys will take the time to answer your questions!

What are the red flags that they need to be aware of that might signal the lawyer is not handling their case properly?

Bad attorneys promise the moon, but are unresponsive to clients' questions, phone calls and correspondence, requests for meetings, etc.

Bad attorneys demand payment in full up front, and then add the statement, "plus additional fees" related to going to trial. This typically means they have no intention of going to trial with your case, but will simply urge, if not coerce, you into a plea bargain.

Bad attorneys insist their client plea bargain and become huffy and even angry when the client insists on going to court. Going to trial means they'll actually have to work for their money!

The list goes on, of course, but those are some pretty clear signs that the attorney is not going to fairly represent you.

In addition to the indicators of "bad attorneys," it truly behooves a defendant and their supporters to become familiar with the legal process. Without knowing what *should be* happening in court, it is almost impossible to know when the attorney is not honestly or fairly representing you.

This was the case with my co-author, Phillip Yow, whose constitutional rights (all three of those mentioned above) were blatantly violated throughout his entire court process and even afterward when attempting to appeal his conviction.

We have all been raised to believe that our judicial system is there to mete out "justice." Unfortunately over the decades the judicial system (criminal and civil) has become a political hot bed in which the participants—judges and attorneys—vie for votes and money. To do that they must scratch each other's backs and in reality—pad each other's pockets. For example, when a judge appoints an attorney to represent a defendant who has no money to pay (a "court-appointed attorney") you can bet that judge will appoint a friend and most often the two will have a back room agreement to coerce the defendant into a quick plea bargain. The attorney-friend will pocket a tidy sum for representing the client, but will have done little to no work to earn even that small pro bono lawyer's fee.

The system has become horribly biased in favor of the rich. Therefore it has also become biased against racial minorities who are usually the ones in lower economic classes.

The judicial system is powerful and intimidating and most people caught in its clutches are too fearful to speak up for themselves. Besides, they don't know the law, so they assume the judge and attorney are playing fairly! Therefore those without large sums of money to fight their cases will be literally railroaded into plea bargained convictions and excessive sentences. The only possible effective weapon is to learn the law.

What are the pitfalls that both the family and defendant need to be aware of when posting bail and dealing with the bail bondsman? Explain what happens when the bail is too high and the judge will not lower it. What should they know about the bail bondsman? Explain why he is not their friend and what his goals are?

The bondsman is essentially the insurance company *for the court*. They are "insuring" that the defendant will show up for their court hearings. They do absolutely nothing for the defendant—except of course take their money.

If a defendant does not show up for a court hearing and cannot be readily found, the bondsman must pay the full amount of the bond to the court. Whether it's a five thousand dollar bond or a million dollar bond, they must pay *all* of it to the court. So, of course they are very protective of *their money!* They will do everything in their power to locate the defendant so they won't have to pay that entire sum of money, and they could care less who they have to harass, threaten, intimidate, and incarcerate to get their money!

For this reason it is wise *never* to sign a bail bond for someone unless you are willing to be incarcerated if *they* don't show up for court. And of course, even then *you* have to pay the bondsman the entire amount of the bond! His *only* goal is to protect his own money!

The court sets the amount for bail, most often leaning toward the amount requested by the district attorney. The defense attorney should be doing all they can to get the lowest possible bond, while the district attorney is fighting for the highest amount. If the court sets a bond that is too high for the defendant to pay, they can request a bond reduction hearing. If the bond remains too high for the defendant to pay, of course they will remain in jail throughout their entire court process.

What are the basics of a pre-trial hearing?

All legal procedures are very complicated, but simply put, pre-trial hearings are intended to be conferences with the judge before the actual trial in the case. The parties to the case are supposed to lay out their evidence and the defendant decides whether to accept a plea bargain if one is offered or whether they will go to trial. If they decide to go to trial they also indicate whether they want to have a trial by jury or whether they want only the judge to hear the case. Once all of these preliminary decisions are made a date is set for an actual trial (sometimes referred to as a "court hearing.")

Within the first section you vividly explain the term plea bargain: First: can you define it for our listeners, and second, can you explain why their family member of a defendant needs to look long and hard before accepting a plea and what the ramifications are?

A plea bargain is an agreement negotiated between the defense attorney and the state's attorney (district attorney) for a certain sentence, if the defendant pleads guilty to the charges against them.

As occurred in my co-author Phillip Yow's case, the defendant may be promised a specific sentence by the attorney representing them which may sound preferable than the sentence that may occur if they insist on going to trial. If the defendant refuses the plea bargain sentence that is offered, most often the attorney will continue to intimidate and coerce them to sign a plea bargain agreement form. Unfortunately, if the defendant still insists on going to trial, the judge and even one's own attorney, as well as the district attorney, will often retaliate, often resulting in a much more severe sentence than that which was offered in the plea bargain. It is a double-edged sword; the best bet is to demand a jury trial, if the defendant refuses the plea bargain.

If the defendant signs that plea bargain form they are admitting guilt. However, even when the defendant accepts the plea bargain the judge does not have to accept it. For example, Phillip's attorney promised him what is called "deferred adjudication probation" if he signed the plea bargain agreement. While he accepted that offer, through a series of subsequent violations of his constitutional rights he did not receive that probation—the judge sentenced him to sixty years in prison and assured he would not be able to appeal it.

It's a long, complicated story, but we are now seeking clemency for Phillip's sentence to be reduced to the time he has already served in prison—fourteen years. We will be posting the progress of this on our website: Prisoner's Family & Friends United (www.pffunited.org) for those who might like to see the process and the ultimate outcome.

Another word of caution: No attorney can "promise" any outcome of a court hearing.

In Phillip's case, his court appointed defense attorney went one step further in deceiving him by writing the words "Open Plea" on the Plea Bargain Agreement form, after Phillip had signed with the belief that he would receive probation.

An "Open Plea" is *not* a "plea bargain." In an "Open Plea" the defendant is literally throwing themselves on the mercy of the court—essentially saying to the judge, "Do whatever you want with me."

When Phillip's attorney wrote those words on the plea bargain form, he created an ambiguous document that allowed the judge to ignore the purported agreement for probation and do whatever he wanted with Phillip—and he did.

Who benefits and why? When a defendant is afraid of going to trial and both the DA and judge realize they are vulnerable, how can a family member or members step in to help? What role should a good and honest lawyer play at this point?

Plea bargains are used to drive fear into the defendant with the more unscrupulous attorneys hammering away at the "fact" that IF the defendant goes to trial they very likely will get a very long sentence, making it sound much better to accept the "shorter" sentence offered in the plea bargain.

Unfortunately, the entire purpose of using plea bargains is to quickly and cheaply clear the court docket, by saving time and avoiding the expense to the court of a lengthy trial. The court benefits; not the defendant.

Plea bargains are not intended to help the defendant—they are intended to help the court. In fact, if every defendant demanded a trial the courts would be so backlogged with cases they could never possibly hear them all in our lifetime! Therefore, only about 2% of all court cases actually go to trial. The other 98% are plea-bargained, despite what our Constitution says about the right to a fair trial.

It is the constitutional *right* of the defendant to have a fair trial by an impartial jury, whether the Court or district attorney or even the defense attorney likes it or not. The problem is that while it is the defendant's *right*, that right is often disregarded in favor of backroom deals by the legal officials who collusively collaborate against the defendant, because he or she has bothered those officials by making them work for their money—and they retaliate.

Why would the courts prefer no trial? Explain the steps in a trial. What are the five things they should know as outlined on pages 38-40?

I've at least partially answered the first part of this question above. However, trials are very expensive for the court and take a great deal of time, thus holding off other cases that need to be processed.

The court process is lengthy and complicated, which is why we devoted such a large portion of the book to walking the reader through the entire process step by step. To do this topic justice, it really requires that some time be devoted to studying the process in

depth, so here I will only summarize briefly what a defendant might experience if they go to trial.

It begins with a magistrate's hearing to read the charges and essentially start the process. A date for trial to determine guilt or innocence will be set. Although the different states vary somewhat, most of the time the defendant has the option of having their case heard by the judge alone or having a jury hear their case.

There will be many delays, especially due to the overcrowding of the court docket. However, if the defendant is found guilty either by an actual trial or a plea bargain, the process will progress to the sentencing phase at the conclusion of which the defendant will receive his or her sentence.

When a conviction is handed down what are the steps needed for an appeal and what should the defendant expect to happen and why?

As with the trial process, the appeal process is extremely complex and must be done in a very timely manner and most often requires a different attorney than the trial attorney—an appellant attorney. The complexity of this process, like the trial process, really requires in depth understanding, therefore, I can only briefly address it here.

When a defendant disagrees with the finding of guilt and/or the sentence given, they have the right to appeal it. There are specific steps that are denoted by law, including filing for a new trial with the same court that first heard the case. If that is not granted, and it rarely is, the defendant embarks on a tedious and lengthy process of filing writs appealing the case. First they apply at the state level, and if the state courts refuse the case the defendant may file a writ at the federal level. Of course, ultimately a case can go to the Supreme Court, if the appeal is not granted at a lower level.

A very important thing to be noted here is that because appeals are generally not granted at the lower levels, they must go to the federal level to ever be heard.

In 1996 Congress passed a law (the Antiterrorism and Effective Death Penalty Act — AEDPA) limiting the time for filing an appeal at the federal level to only one year following the defendant's conviction.

The reason this is so critical is because it is impossible for a prisoner to ever meet that deadline. First of all, most prisoners are not well versed in the law, so the first thing they must do is learn the law. Well, it takes attorneys many years of study…graduate school, interning, and finally passing the bar, before they engage in fighting cases in court, let alone appealing convictions—and law students and fledgling attorneys have ready access to state of the art law libraries twenty-four hours a day. Prisoners do not have that luxury.

By law, all prisons have law libraries. However, a prisoner may request to go to the law library at the prison, but the prison does not have to grant them that request, and even when it is granted it may only be for an hour or so a week, and in most cases the legal resources are limited and often out of date. Therefore the prisoner cannot possibly learn the law and learn how to prepare a writ and get it filed in sufficient time to meet the one-year, AEDPA imposed time limit for filing a federal writ in pursuit of overturning their conviction. When that happens, their case is time-barred from ever being heard.

While there are incidents in which a prisoner was able to successfully appeal their own case—referred to as filing "pro se," it takes many, many years to do so—fifteen or twenty. Therefore, unless a prisoner—or their family—is extremely wealthy and has access to virtually endless amounts of money to pay appellant attorneys, the typical prisoner will remain confined to prison as sentenced by the lower court, without any remedy.

Here it is important to point out that tragically ten's of thousands of prisoners who are incarcerated today are actually innocent. The National Innocence Project that has effectively freed almost 400 innocent prisoners—some from death row—since the 1980s reports the belief that approximately 5% of prisoners are innocent. They point out that if *only* 1% of today's prisoners were innocent that would be 20,000+ innocent people who are falsely incarcerated and unable to be freed from prison. Multiply that by even 5% and you have an entire city of people who are innocent sitting in prison today.

Explain the sentencing procedure and the appeal procedure, and why appeals can drag on.

Well, like all of the criminal justice process the sentencing procedure is also complex. It is not as complicated on paper as it is in practice. For example, most offenses have a fixed sentencing schedule, if you will. For a certain crime the state statutes might ascribe a sentence of five years to sixty years, and the judge is to determine where within that range they will sentence the defendant.

Sentencing is supposed to be based on the circumstances surrounding the offense: the defendant's mental condition, extenuating circumstances such as being under the influence of drugs or alcohol, etc. However sentencing has also become a political tool for many judges who believe they will win more votes by appearing "tough on crime," so they often ascribe the toughest sentence (regardless of any mitigating circumstances) just to look "tough on crime." Thus, sentencing becomes extremely unjust and unfair.

With regard to the appellate process "dragging on," that is largely because once a writ is filed with an appellate court they have no defined time limit within which to respond to the defendant. Innocent people have waited ten or more years for a response from an appellate court, only to be later found innocent after sitting in prison extraordinary lengths of time, even thirty or forty years.

Why does this affect not only the prisoner but the family too? Why is a stigma attached to them and what happens when members of their community

learn about their family member's incarceration? Why do some just deny it and claim the person is on vacation or in school?

There is a saying that "the prisoner does time on the inside while the family does time on the outside."

When a loved one enters prison they are actually entering a foreign culture and they virtually take their family with them into that new culture. Everyone must adapt.

In large part to support the prison family, the organization of which I am director initiated and annually holds the National Prisoner's Family Conference. Our 6th annual conference will be held February 19-21, 2014 in Dallas, Texas. There are presentations and workshops on many of the issues uniquely affecting prison families, as well as on understanding the prison culture and how it affects the prisoner and their family.

Emotionally, what affects the prisoner also affects those who love them. If you really care about a prisoner—say your spouse, your son or daughter, your parent—you experience their pain. When you learn how unjustly and inhumanely they are treated in prison you feel the misery they experience. This compounds the emotions of grief that you are already experiencing.

Additionally, the loss of a loved one to prison impacts the family tangibly. Quite often the loved one who is incarcerated was a primary breadwinner for the family. Once they are incarcerated they can no longer provide support to the family; in fact, in most cases families financially support the prisoner.

The cynical citizen surmises the prisoner has it easy—"3 hots and a cot," not a worry in the world. The reality is that prisons are dangerous places where the prisoner must be on guard every minute to avoid violence that might erupt, and despite popular thought, prisons do not provide prisoners with the basic necessities for living.

In most prisons, while prisoners are required to work—even required to do work that brings income into the prison—they are either paid absolutely nothing (as is the case here in Texas) or they are paid ten cents or a quarter an hour. Then they must pay for their necessities.

Yes—there is a roof over their heads. And, yes, almost always three less-than-nutritious meals a day are provided. However, some prisons even make prisoners pay for sheets for their cot; other prisons require prisoners to pay for their uniforms, underwear, socks and shoes; most prisons do not provide basic hygiene items, such as toothpaste—and the list goes on. In those cases, the prisoner's family must pay, by putting money into the prisoner's account so they can have the necessities needed for daily survival.

If families want to talk with their loved one in prison, they must pay—often an outrageous charge—at least 3.00 for a 15 or 20-minute phone call (plus service charges) and that quickly adds up. Even if the family wants to receive letters from the prisoner, the prisoner must purchase writing materials and postage stamps...which the family must pay for.

Travel for visitation is extremely costly, which is why the majority of prisoners receive no visits.

The financial cost to the prison family is extraordinary, resulting in many who never received welfare in their lives becoming dependent upon public assistance.

The emotional cost of a loved one's incarceration exceeds grief and constant fear that their loved one is safe in a very dangerous environment. For far too long the prison family has been disdained equally as much as the prisoner. They are often shunned by society; frequently blamed for their loved ones errors.

Besides, prison is known as a place "bad people" go...so families, including the children, tend to isolate and withdraw from the mainstream community in shame and embarrassment that their loved one has done a terrible deed. Very often, in their shame, they create cover stories for the absence of their loved one...they are away in school; they've joined the military; they've started working as a long haul trucker... avoiding the shame and embarrassment of having a loved one in prison.

Somewhat of a digression, but I recently heard this from someone who works with prisoners:

A little boy brought home a spelling assignment and his father asked him what the first word was on his spelling list.

The little boy replied, "Prison."

The father responded, "Prison. That's a very bad place where bad people go when they do bad things."

The little boy stared at his father with a puzzled look on his face as if expecting additional information.

Finally, the little boy broke the silence and asked, "Daddy, if prison is where bad people go when they do bad things, where do good people go when they do bad things?"

The fact is that there are many good, intelligent, talented people confined in our prisons, but the word "prison" itself conjures up the very worst about them.

Explain the chain of grief: Denial, anger, bargaining, depression and acceptance and how does a person work through it?

Initially, the members of the prison family are thrust into grief when learning of their loved one's arrest — as is the prisoner, too.

As early as the 1950s a psychiatrist, Elisabeth Kubler Ross, developed the grief cycle out of her lifelong study on death and dying. It has never been refuted and is used routinely by all helping professionals in addressing "loss."

When a person is arrested, they have obviously lost their freedom and often continue to lose all else that is dear to them—their job, their house, their car, their friends—even their family. For example, those with children not only lose them physically, but in many cases parental rights are taken from them com-

pletely—legally terminated. Prisoners grieve those losses.

The prisoner's loved ones have experienced loss as well. Obviously they have lost a family member; they can no longer pick up the phone and call them at will, have them over for Sunday dinner, depend on them for financial support or even emotional support. They grieve that loss.

The entire family has lost their former way of life and for the most part their lives will never be the same. Typically they don't recognize that they are experiencing grief, as they close the former chapter of their lives.

Grief and how we handle it is different for each of us. But typically once we have accepted that the loss is permanent, we move from denial through anger that the loss has occurred and bounce between anger and bargaining with God in an attempt to get our loved one—and even our old life—back.

When the permanency of the loss becomes very real to us, we are typically plunged into a deep depression.

The stages of grief are not fixed, because we bounce back and forth through each stage forever...we even return to denial years after a loss...but ultimately most people resolve their grief by accepting the loss as real and adapting to a new way of life, incorporating the loss into their daily activities.

Time truly does help us resolve the grief. While sadness and tears may unexpectedly spring forth, over time it becomes easier to manage the loss and learn a new way to live.

The emotional impact of incarceration ultimately results in posttraumatic stress for each member of the prison family.

These emotion-related topics are so critical that a good number of workshops are devoted to addressing them at the Prisoner's Family Conference.

What effect does this have on children and why do they feel that they are not worthy of love, act out

and feel isolated too? How can this be prevented and what are ways to make these children feel wanted? What should never be said of discussed in front of them and why?

Perhaps children are more traumatized by the loss of a loved one to prison than the adults, and that is because not only are the adults immersed in their own grief and unable to recognize that the children are truly traumatized and grieving too, but adults often believe that children are "too young to understand." So, they leave the children out of any discussions about the loss.

When children (or any of us, for that matter) have no appropriate outlets for their pain and fears, they begin acting out their emotions—becoming rebellious or even physically aggressive; turning to drugs and alcohol to numb the pain, etc.—and thus they begin their own plunge into problematic behaviors.

It is critical for people to understand that children, even infants, experience a profound sense of loss and grief when a loved one is incarcerated. The topic should be discussed openly in a language children can understand and never in a manner that belittles or degrades the incarcerated loved one.

If the incarcerated loved one is a blood relative, especially if they are a parent, children are fully aware that they are the product of that person—they not only carry their genes, but they have been emotionally and mentally formed by the lost person. So when anyone says degrading things about the prisoner they are literally—especially to the child—indicating that the child has those same negative traits. The criticism hurled at the prisoner actually lands on the child and ultimately becomes a permanent part of their self-awareness—their self-esteem.

It's not that we should never argue or complain in front of children. That would paint a picture of an unrealistic world. But when children are listening, our disagreements and complaints should be sensitively aired. This is such an impor-

tant issue that several workshops at the Prisoner's Family Conference are devoted to this topic. For those who may be interested the conference visit www.prisonersfamilyconference.org.

When a person is transferred to a prison they become as you state: property of the prison. After reading this book and understanding what happens at this point, not only do they lose the right to make any decisions about their lives, what they eat, drink or when they sleep but they lose the their dignity and are often denied the basics needed to live. How can we make the public understand that they are human beings, some are innocent and that many just want to serve their time, get out and be with their family again? What needs to be done to change the mindset of those running the prison? Property is defined as: Things belonging to someone, or something tangible or intangible to which its owner has legal title: a person is tangible; a person in prison has not given over a title to allow others to mistreat them and be treated as something someone bought: How should this be changed?

Unfortunately, prison has become a huge and very lucrative industry in our country. In fact, the United States is the largest jailer in the entire world; with only 5% of the world's population we incarcerate a full 25% of the entire world's prisoners.

Prison was never intended to become a business in which human beings would become be the inventory. Prison was intended to remove dangerous people from society—keeping society safe, but also providing an opportunity for the offender to reflect and change their "errant ways."

The word "penitentiary" is derived from the word "penitence" meaning to reflect on one's wrong doings and correct one's errors in thinking. In fact the first prison in this country—established in the early 1800's in Pennsylvania, was founded on religious principles, whereby those who offended against society were essentially housed there to give penance for their wrong doings.

Well, somewhere along the line someone—or several someones—realized a financial profit could be made by warehousing human beings, leading to the mass incarceration we have in this country today.

Additionally, criminal justice as a whole is now a tool of politicians—judges are elected; district attorneys are elected; prison directors are appointed by elected governors and so on.

In 1976 these politicians decided it sounded good to wage "war on drugs." They obviously thought that looking tough on crime would gain votes.

The truth is that from day one, the War on Drugs has been an utter failure, but it sounded good to the general public, so it became a political tool, i.e. "I'll get those drug-criminals off our streets, if you elect me."

But drugs are everywhere today in greater quantities than ever, and what do we have to show for it?

Eighty percent of our prisoners today—*80%*—are non-violent drug offenders...kids who sold a bag of marijuana to help the family put food on the table; mothers who carried a brown paper sack for their boyfriend. The drug cartels—the dangerous drug lords with arsenals of weapons—are alive and well, and for the most part insulated from legal repercussions, while the small often innocent citizen is warehoused in a prison.

There's a chart in our book *The Unvarnished Truth about the Prison Family Journey* that depicts just how the population of our prisons escalated almost overnight as a result of the drug war our politicians thought would make them sound like they actually cared about the citizens. But what those politicians actually did was to take the control of our legal system out of the hands of citizens and place it firmly into the hands of politicians who have corrupted the initial intent of incarceration by making it a lucrative business to pad their own pockets. They make the rules to assure criminal justice is lucrative for them, and some of those rules are outrageous and even dangerous.

Most people are unaware that the growing privatization of prisons is dangerous. Most people are unaware that the growing privatization of prisons is making a few people very rich—The American Corrections Corporation and GEO (the two largest private prison corporations in the world) are on the *stock exchange*; it's so lucrative that one Wall Street broker invested $9 *million* dollars in *one* New York private prison.

Those companies rake in billions of dollars annually for warehousing prisoners. It's a business.

To be successful in business their industry must *grow*. To grow, these businesses spend millions of dollars each year lobbying our legislators for prisoners—more prisoners means more money. Private prison operators demand that their private prisons remain at 90% capacity for twenty years before they sign a contract with a state to warehouse their prisoners. What other industry can make such a demand? What if private hospitals demanded their hospital beds remain at 90% capacity for twenty years?

Business is business and to remain lucrative the private prisons must be profitable. They do that by cutting corners—feeding prisoners on $3 a day; making prisoners buy their own sheets and clothing; shutting off water and electricity in the cell areas for extended periods of time; turning off hot water to the showers; and the list goes on and on.

The best thing we can do to ever stop this blight on our society is to inform the unaware citizen; openly talk about these things. Last year at the national Prisoner's Family Conference attendees initiated the End Mass Incarceration Movement. We put it on Facebook and it exploded like wildfire. We now have End Mass Incarceration chapters in many states; all are doing their part to educate the public that we must take our concerns to our legislators and demand prison reform.

Why is there no accountability in prisons, why can a judge make his/her own rules?

Because politicians control every aspect of our criminal justice system they have assured that there is absolutely no independent oversight of the entire criminal justice system—including everything from law enforcement officers on the street to our courtrooms and our prisons. Politicians, especially those who have invested heavily in the industry, do not want anyone to interfere with their lucrative business. Thus, prisons are self-regulated—even juvenile prisons.

Are you aware that there is absolutely no independent oversight of the juvenile detention facilities? I had that rude awakening while working at a private juvenile facility in Colorado, where on the first day of my new job I found the juveniles being physically abused by the staff. I quit my job within six months and attempted to report the abuse to Child Protective Services. Imagine my shock and dismay when they informed me that detention facilities, whether adult or juvenile, are self-regulated and no outside entity has the *right* to investigate what is going on behind their locked doors. No one can just walk into any detention facility and say, "I just want to look around."

Ultimately, only by going to the media (which truly took a genuine interest in that Colorado facility) was the abuse ever disclosed publicly, and there came such a huge outcry that the facility was finally closed.

There is absolutely no independent oversight of our criminal justice system, and the business-people operating that system will do everything they can to avoid any oversight, including degrading and humiliating anyone who makes a move to confront their practices.

For example, when I advocate on behalf of a prisoner, wardens rarely return my calls, and when they do they respond by telling me I'm "foolish" and even "stupid" to ever believe anything any prisoner tells me.

I have known my co-author, Phillip Yow, for almost twenty-five years, and in that time he has never once lied to me—not once—about anything at all. So, when he tells me an officer has brutalized or humiliated himself or a fellow prisoner, I have no reason not to believe him—in fact, he is the first person to tell me that "some of these people belong in prison." But, when I take the grievance to the warden of the prison, before I can get the words out of my mouth they will say, "That's a lie."

They do that to get rid of me. They don't want anyone looking at what is going on at the prison. In fact, prisoners are disciplined for telling an outsider of the brutality and inhumane treatment they experience. Do you know that it is almost harder for an outsider to get *into* a prison than it is for a prisoner to get out (I mean, escape.)?

So, when advocating, while I always expect prisoners to follow the rules, especially when reporting grievances, and I always follow the prison's expected protocol for outsiders reporting grievances, when the issue is extremely serious I take it to my state representative, whose office has always been very supportive.

In a recent visit to their office, the representative's aide told me that the representative had repeatedly asked the director of our state prison system to provide an accounting of the cost for keeping a prisoner in solitary confinement in comparison to keeping a prisoner in the general population of the prison. For over a year the representative and her aides attempted to get this seemingly simple information, but were stonewalled from receiving it—a *state representative*; in fact, a *state representative on the state's criminal justice committee*—and the prison refused to give them the information—and they don't have to! The prisons are accountable to no one, and they intend to keep it that way. That's how tightly the administrators guard their empire and protect their six-figure salaries. It is an outrage.

What are the best modes of communication and how can family members be assured that their letters are given to the person in prison? Why are

phone calls often the best way to communicate and why would they disallow a visit?

Actually, we can never be sure our correspondence is received by a prisoner, until they respond and tell us that it was. But, the truth is that in our experience we haven't actually had any real problems with written correspondence ending up—eventually—where it belonged!

However, when a person is incarcerated prison staff monitors all forms of communication. Staff is actually hired specifically to read all correspondence going in and out of prisons; phone calls are recorded. Therefore communication remains very guarded unless the family is allowed face-to-face visitation with the prisoner—which therefore is actually the best way to have open communication with the prisoner. Unfortunately, contact visits are not allowed for all prisoners, so often visitation takes place through a glass and on phones that are monitored.

Unfortunately, most families cannot afford to visit the prisons anyhow. The typical prisoner in the United States is housed over 500 miles away from their home, making visitation extremely expensive for the family. For example, the few times I have visited Phillip over the years, each visit cost me at least $500...and believe me, that's *not* because I choose the most luxurious forms of travel and lodging and eat out at five-star restaurants!

But to travel the more than 500 miles from my home to his prison requires gasoline or a plane ticket and rental car (for which I must purchase gasoline), and at least three nights in a motel. Although I choose lodging with a microwave and refrigerator in the room—bringing some food and supplies with me or purchasing them when I arrive—I must come into town the day before visitation and then stay overnight to visit the second day. If I drive, I spend a third night in the motel and leave the next morning for the 500+ mile drive home. Even if I fly, I may need to spend that

third night in a motel, because visitation hours and flight schedules are not always compatible.

But, being fair, unfortunately, there actually is a need for the prison to oversee prisoners' communication, because there are those people in prison who are devious and will plot and plan with outsiders to break out or bring in various forms of contraband. However, the average prisoner just wants to do their time and get out and back to their life in the community. Unfortunately, the few bad apples really do spoil things for the whole barrel!

Explain what should be expected if they are allowed to visit and why things take so long?

Visitation is extremely stressful both emotionally and logistically.

Logistically visitors can be expected to be thoroughly searched and patted down. Typically the officers are reasonably amiable, but often there is one or more who can be very curt and even rude to visitors.

Lines into visitation areas can be very long—I've waited over an hour to just get into the door to be searched...and by the time the prisoner gets to the visitation area from their cell it could be another hour. Almost always the process is very slow, not to mention very intimidating and stressful. You really cannot relax until the person you have come to visit is in your sight and seated and talking with you.

Visiting time passes quickly and emotionally speaking the most painful time is ending the visit—when you must leave the prisoner behind and return to the uncaring community, where you must pretend that everything is fine, when in your heart you know everything is *not* fine—you've just left someone you care deeply about behind in a cage.

How can a family prepare when their loved one is being released? How are they accepted or not accepted and what happens when they seek work?

Ideally, preparation for re-entry should begin the moment a person is arrested. But, that is highly unrealistic. Therefore, once a prisoner is settled into their primary if not permanent prison unit, the family should be having serious talks about what went wrong and what must be different for the prisoner to succeed when they return to the community.

It doesn't matter how long the sentence is—you can't wait until weeks or days before a prisoner is released to adequately prepare for a successful re-entry. The prisoner must take advantage of each day in prison to prepare for their return, and the family must similarly prepare themselves for the family reunification.

We have a very thorough section of *The Unvarnished Truth about the Prison Family Journey* devoted to community re-entry and family reunification, and it includes understanding family dynamics and how family members affect one another.

One of the greatest fallacies is for a family to place all of the blame on the prisoner for being incarcerated and all of the responsibility on the prisoner for succeeding when they return home. A prisoner is a member of a family; a family is a system in which one part—one member—affects all of the other parts, or members of that system. To be most effective each member of that system much search themselves for answers to what went wrong and how they can improve things in the future.

In our book we provide an extensive list of what to expect for six years after a prisoner has returned to the community.

Logistically the most challenging aspect of re-entry is that prisoners are certainly not welcomed back by the larger community. Although there's been some improvement lately, most job applications ask whether the applicant has a felony record. If the applicant lies and says "No," when they've just come out of prison, they can readily be fired if the employer ever learns they do have a felony. If the applicant says, "Will discuss in person," they'll never get an inter-

view, because that's a dead give-away that the answer is "Yes."

Public housing and rental agencies, by law, may not rent to felons. So, housing becomes a critical issue for returning prisoners.

Of course, most prisoners leave prison with a few dollars and the clothes on their back, and most have no source of income for a very long time after their release. So, unless they have strong family support they have no means to even get food to eat, let alone necessities for living. Some end up in homeless shelters; others end up in the streets, and 85% return to prison as a result. We must have stronger re-entry programs for returning prisoners. Some ministries are providing support, but not enough.

Explain the effect this has on children as described in the chapter: Children of Prisoners

We talked earlier about the effects of a loved one's incarceration on children in the family. But, when a parent returns from prison the children are strongly affected.

Throughout the parents' (or other loved one's) lengthy absence, the child has lost a great deal of trust in the relationship. They fear trusting again. Once trust is broken it is extremely hard to re-build.

I recall one ten year old girl who refused to go to school after her mother returned from about five years in prison. At first the child claimed she was sick, but when nothing was found to be wrong with her, we decided to do some informal counseling.

What I learned was the child did not want her mother out of her sight; she thought that she could stop her mother from doing anything wrong that might result in her mother being incarcerated again. The thought of going to school and leaving her mother "without supervision" was literally terrifying to this little girl. I'm sure many children have similar feelings.

Children have grown and matured in their parents' absence, often taking on major roles in the family. When the parent comes home, the child isn't

91

prepared to give up their new role to let the return-ing parent take over. This often leads to disagreements and arguments about who is in charge in the family.

Re-entry and family reunification are covered in a number of presentations and workshops at the national Prisoner's Family Conference. We encourage prison families to attend, but we also encourage coun-selors and educators and ministry volunteers and oth-ers who work with children and families of prisoners to attend to learn how best to help these families dur-ing and following a loved one's incarceration.

Within the chapter "The Prison System" you tell it all and everyone needs to hear it: Costs of using the infirmary, cost to the prison for meals, trust funds for prisoners, use of the commissary, injustices in this system and your discussion with the warden. It's very enlightening. How can the public and the right agencies change this? Many think that prison-ers receive these great meals, medical care, and the basic necessities in life. Why don't they, and how can we make the public more aware of this mistreat-ment? Who are the people that might listen, and when you have your conference what information to you give to the families that attend to empower them?

Actually, the goal of the Prisoner's Family Conference is to empower prison families.

To be empowered the first thing that anyone must do is to become educated—knowledge truly is power. The conference provides excellent education and resources on all of the things that affect prison families legally and emotionally. We've had attendees who've told us they've learned more in this three-day conference than they learned in years of working with prisoners and their families and we've had prison fam-ily members who were so encouraged and supported by the conference and the information they receive there that they regret having waited to come—and now attend every year.

The conference is a wonderful resource in and of itself. We strongly encourage anyone who wants to learn and wishes to do more to empower prison fami-lies—including prison family members themselves—to attend.

It concerns me that more educators do not attend. One in every seven school children has a parent either in prison, on probation, or parole. An enormous number of children are affected, yet few educators are aware of this fact, let alone aware of how to help the child of a prisoner.

Very few criminal justice professionals attend, although we actively reach out to them. Their mindset is so closed that they only understand "control" and have no concern for the children and families of pris-oners. This is very wrong, and we will continue to do all we can to reach out and educate them—one by one if necessary.

The last section is a real eye opener, as it was written by the co-author of this book who is serving time. Describe how Phillip discusses prisoner safety and the way some prisoners fall prey to gangs. What are the warning signs, how do they scope them out, and why are so many reeled in by them? What makes them think they are part of a family when they are basically using them for their own purpose?

Phillip very candidly wrote about subjects that are taboo for prisoners to share outside the prison walls. He firmly believes that keeping the truth from the public is what allows the inhumane treatment of prisoners and even the violence in prison to continue unabated.

One interesting experience happened after the book was published and Phillip was sharing it with other inmates. A gang member read the book and brought it back to Phillip, saying, "I don't like what you've written in here about prison gangs...but, it's the truth!"

Phillip is extremely opposed to gangs of all kinds, but especially to prison gangs, because they are the source of much violence in prison. Gangs intimidate new prisoners…weaker prisoners…to join by promising them protection, and naively they join. But, the gang will quickly turn on a member they believe has betrayed them in any way, brutally assaulting and even killing the perceived enemy in the blink of an eye without a second thought. Unfortunately, I've now heard of these routine assaults and murders more times than I can count. I can't imagine what it must be like to witness them first-hand on almost a daily basis. Typically the prison will pass the deaths off as "suicides," so I always question such reports.

In the book Phillip addresses the best ways prisoners can avoid gangs and other problems. However he especially emphasizes how important the family is to the prisoner; how critical it is that the family emotionally support the prisoner and encourage the prisoner to do the right thing regardless of what they see going on around them. Family involvement can actually help to keep a prisoner safe. For the most part, prisoners without strong family support don't do well in prison.

What are the two purposes and what should a prisoner do if they do not want to join a gang, and how do they do this, if at all possible, without being harmed? Why won't the guards, the warden, or prison officials protect the prisoners? Why do they look away?

New prisoners are recruited by prison gangs to be used for monetary and sexual gain by the gang members. Gang members are very deceptive, so they recruit those they perceive as weak by using the ploy that the new prisoner-recruit will be safe if they join the gang—the gang will "protect" them.

Even though it's frightening, the best thing a prisoner can do to avoid being recruited by a gang is to firmly and consistently say "No" when gang members try to recruit them.

You ask why the guards and other prison officials won't protect the inmates. Well, the prison policy (written and unwritten) is that they are there to protect the public from the prisoners, not to protect the prisoners from each other. Therefore, they do not intervene in incidents of violence.

Prison staff doesn't even intervene to take care of the wounded; that becomes the responsibility of the other prisoners as well. It's a bloody horror show in real time. And, it's not only the prisoners who are violent; the guards are equally as violent, and often with little or no provocation. If they've had a bad day, or just want to assert their power, they'll viciously verbally and physically humiliate and assault prisoners. Prison is a dangerous place.

When violence erupts or misconduct arises, how does a prisoner fight back? What are the pitfalls of the grievance process, and why doesn't it serve to help the person who fills out the forms? Why are wardens allowed to stamp their responses, and why at the second level is the response the same? How can a prisoner fight for safety if no one cares or listens? Where do they go and how can families be heard?

Of course, prisoners should avoid violence if at all possible. However, if their life is in jeopardy, of course they must do what they have to do to remain safe. Many a prisoner will tell you that it became necessary to physically fight to "prove" themselves. But, once other prisoners learn they will do what is necessary to protect themselves, others became less and less aggressive toward them. They eventually establish a pecking order and develop a reputation.

When any form of misconduct occurs in prison there is a standard protocol staff is expected is to follow. (They may or may not follow it.)

Depending on how serious the infraction is, the guards will write an incident report and give a "case" or "ticket" to the offending inmate. That is supposed to be followed with a hearing at which the prisoner can refute or accept the charges. Then the prison administration determines the punishment. The punishment does not always fit the "crime." It could range from losing privileges, such as use of the phones or rec yard, to lengthy stays in isolation.

Prisons have a grievance process. If the prisoner believes they've been treated unjustly they can file a written grievance, but in reality most prisoners—especially long time prisoners learn that no matter how justified they are in grieving the "case," the prison maintains its stance, refusing to even consider that the prisoner may be justified. There is no fairness in this process. Everything is weighted on the side of the prison.

Explain the pitfalls of financial support

I mentioned earlier that prisoners with family support rely on their family for money to purchase basic necessities.

In 2009, before our first Prisoner's Family Conference, I engaged two long-time prisoners in writing a manual that would provide really good information on what a prisoner needs from their family to do well during their incarceration. One of the authors of that manual actually developed an extensive survey and distributed it to 100 prisoners at his unit. Seventy prisoners responded.

The responses to one of the questions surprised me.

The question was, "How much money do you need from your family each month to survive in prison?"

About 10% of the respondents said they didn't need any money; they felt they had already burdened their family enough just by being in prison. About 5% said they needed $75-$100 a month to be "comfortable" in prison. The other 85% said they only needed $25-$35 a month to take care of "necessities."

The fact is that a prisoner can survive in prison with no money. It's tough, but they can survive. Unfortunately, with no money they will likely resort to unscrupulous measures—gambling, sexual favors and the like—to get their needs met. If a family can provide between $25 and $50 a month, a prisoner will be safer and do much better.

However, when a prisoner asks for large sums of money, or asks their family to put money in another inmate's account, you can pretty well know that the prisoner is being extorted—they're being threatened to pay for protection or they have a huge gambling debt they haven't been able to pay—in other words, they are in danger.

Explain: Effective communication as it is described in this section, and why do prisoners often feel alone when they lack letters, any kind of communication with their family, and why do some family members divorce themselves from this person, and why do some claim they are going to do something for them and never do it?

We'd like to know the answer to the last part of your question, ourselves. We have no idea why people make promises they don't keep! Perhaps they had good intentions and something prevented them from fulfilling the promise. I don't know. But, I do know that it is very hurtful to prisoners when we tell them we're going to do something for them and we don't do it—and especially hurtful when we lie to them, saying we've already done what they asked, when we haven't. No one likes being lied to.

Prisoners are very much alone in prison. To remain safe, they must only look out for themselves and thereby learn to be very selfish.

Prisoners with long sentences generally find that outside support dwindles, actually vanishes over the years. Many families become involved with their own problems and needs and little by little drift away from supporting the prisoner.

But with regard to effectively communicating with prisoners if the family wants to improve relations during a loved ones incarceration, they need to communicate openly and honestly with one another to have the best relationship. No good relationship can be built on deception or lies or even half truths.

Unfortunately, when a person is incarcerated, both the prisoner and the loved ones in the community actually censor information they share with each other: the prisoner keeps secrets about the brutality and hardships of prison life, and the loved ones keep secrets about hardships they are facing. Each seems to think they must protect the other from reality, but what they are doing is attempting to build a relationship on deception—attempting to make each other believe all is well, when it's not.

We can be sensitive about the things we share, but to build a solid relationship it's important to be real with one another. It's important to be able to discuss difficult issues with one another. If you can't talk about real issues and difficulties with a loved one, who can you talk about them with?

What happens when guards and prisoners get too close? Why are so many guards corrupt? How can the public and the right officials change this or can it be changed?

I was recently on a radio show with a gentleman who was a former guard at Rikers Island in New York. He wrote a book—*Corruption Officer*—related to his experience as having engaged in tremendous corruption while serving as a guard and ultimately being caught and incarcerated himself.

Unfortunately, guards engage in corruption, not only because they are not paid well, but because they become greedy...and when they realize they can make thousands of dollars a day, as did this former officer, by bringing contraband into the prisons, they take advantage of it. He was bringing in cigarettes—$50 for ONE cigarette; drugs; cell phones...literally making $1,000-$5,000 a day.

Of course, the prisons primarily blame the visitors and prisoners for such contraband, but it is virtually impossible for a visitor to smuggle in twenty pounds of cocaine or fifty cell phones without being caught.

It is common for guards to have sexual relationships with prisoners—both hetero and homosexual relations. Of course if they're caught, the guard will be fired. But on occasion some of these relations become romantic and the couples even marry. Some female guards have even been heard to say that they took a job at the prison just to find a husband! Most often these relationships don't last.

There are five basic human needs that Phillip describes: Physical comfort, safety, sense of belonging and feeling loved, sense of self-esteem and respect, and the sense of self actualization: Why are prisoners denied all five and what are some ways you are working to change this? Why are their basic hygienic needs denied and what happens when a prisoner has no one to go to and they're really all alone?

The last chapter of *The Unvarnished Truth about the Prison Family Journey* is based on a sound theory developed by well-respected psychologist, Abraham Maslow back in the 1940s. His theory indicates that as humans we all have basic needs that must be fulfilled in order for us to have satisfying, productive lives. Unfortunately, the prison system meets none of those needs. Therefore prisoners remain unfulfilled and dissatisfied with life, often becoming bitter and angry.

The only way those basic human needs can be met for the prisoner, is by their loved ones in the community. That is why the family is so very important to the prisoner's ultimate success, both while incarcerated and when returning to the community.

How can the public learn more about your work, your conference and how to support what you are hoping everyone understands about the Unvarnished Truth about the Prison Family Journey after reading this book? Do you plan to write another one and what will you include in it?

Actually, Phillip and I have discussed a future book, which would include our efforts to seek clemency for the time he has already served in prison. It would include more about advocacy for prisoners and their families and how they can better advocate for themselves.

For our other work, we try to make finding us as easy as possible, so the Prisoner's Family Conference website is simply:

www.prisonersfamilyconference.org

Also, although we haven't fully launched this project, Phillip and I initiated Prisoners' Families and Friends United as an on-line resource for prison families. We will be putting information about our quest to seek clemency for Phillip on that website which is simply www.pffunited.org.

Of course those websites have other contact information such as our phone number and e-mail addresses. We welcome inquiries and attempt to be timely in our responses!

Where can everyone learn more about the conference and where to get this book? What are the documents included at the end of the book that is vital and that every family member should have at their fingertips?

In addition to the Prisoner's Family Conference website there is a Prisoner's Family Conference Facebook page and we encourage those who are on Facebook to "like" our page for on-going information that is helpful to prisoners and their families.

We do include several legal documents in *The Unvarnished Truth about the Prison Family Journey*, such as the power of attorney and release of informa-tion form that are helpful to families when their loved one is incarcerated.

In addition to finding the book on Amazon.com, people can request that their local library and even local bookstores order the book for them. Once it's in the local library others can find this resource, and I might add that *The Unvarnished Truth about the Prison Family Journey* is the only comprehensive resource available for prison families, so it would be great if local libraries had several on their shelves.

What else would you like to add and what questions should family members ask when the initial call comes in and how should they proceed from the start?

Well, I would certainly like to thank you, Fran, for inviting me for this interview. It would have been great if Phillip could have participated, too, because he is extremely articulate in discussing these issues. It is our prayer that our quest for clemency for Phillip will be successful and that he will be able to participate in future interviews, perhaps even within a year. We encourage those who would like to join us in that prayer to do so.

We believe *The Unvarnished Truth about the Prison Family Journey* is a vital resource. We hope that people will read it, not just after they are faced with the daunting journey, but to learn the truth about our criminal justice system and how it truly affects all of us in this country.

Thank you again for this opportunity.

BULLYING

Rev. Faith McDonald

As a child, I was bullied, often. I believe, in some ways I was a target. You see, I was a very sheltered child. My mother and father tried to conceive for thirteen years before becoming pregnant with me. Their ages were, Mother thirty and Father thirty-two when I was born. I was their miracle baby. And then, sixteen months later, my one and only sibling was born, a brother.

The reason I say I was a target was in this wise. Being sheltered, you do not see much of the world for how it truly is. My mother was a stay at home mom until it was time for me to start school. If I went anywhere...she was there. Then, when it came time for me to start school, they started me in a private school. I had so much separation anxiety. I didn't fit in at all! I had red hair and a horrible overbite. I had been taught zero social skills. I was very shy. I blushed if anyone spoke to me and went numb if any undue attention was brought upon me. As sharks smell blood, I believe that bullies smell innocents.

Children would taunt me. Pick me out on the playground to harass. Groups of girls would surround me. I was defenseless. I was never taught how to fight. I was told to be friendly, nice, and kind, which I was by nature; however, these attributes did not seem to serve me well in this social setting.

The bullying continued throughout elementary school, middle school, and high school. By the ninth grade, I quit! You would think that would be the end.

Nothing could be farther from the truth. I was bullied on my jobs, sexually harassed, made to do all the menial tasks, was in abusive relationships...the list goes on and on.

When and where did this life of abuse and bullying stop ? When I realized who I was in Christ. You see...I didn't know who I was. I didn't realize the power available to me. And I learned to "do things afraid." I no longer allowed fear to stop me. I change my perception of self, and by doing so, it changed others' perceptions of me.

Parents can make one of two mistakes. They can shelter too much and not teach their children the tools they need to go into the world well equipped. Or, they can throw them to the wolves, where I believe bullies are created. Balance. Balance is the key. If you have a sensitive child, you may have to better equip them. If you have an extroverted child, or one that fighting comes naturally for, you may have to give them a dose of their own medicine by maybe taking them to a karate class or boxing ring so someone can feed them their lunch, so to speak. I believe it is different for every child. The most important thing is to get them while they're young. Parents...be involved. Don't stick your head in the sand and cause your child to travel these dark roads alone. *Little Red Riding Hood* should have never been walking in the woods alone. And if it were completely necessary for her to do so, mace should have been in the basket. Be aware of your surroundings. If you have a kind heart, don't lose it. However, have wisdom alongside it.

There really were monsters under my bed. Also shadows outside my windows. They were premonitions of things to come. I wish I would have known how strong the forces that were with me were against the forces that were against me. I would have stood taller and with much more confidence, and would have scared some of the bullies away !

Greater is He that is within you, than he that is in the world. 1 John 4:4

————————

Rev. Faith McDonald is President and Co-Pastor of W.H.A.M. Inc.

SPECIAL FOCUS: BULLYING

John Emil Augustine on Bullying

Topics that fall under the umbrella of abuse or bullying are near and dear to me. My hope is to spread the message to those who are being abused, to those who know someone who is being abused, and to those who are abusing that we are here to help and respect each other, we are here to survive each other's abuse, and we are here to learn about and improve ourselves.

I believe abuse is in our nature. We take advantage of each other because we are animals. I don't mean that in a derogatory way. What I mean is when we study our own biology and cognition, we find we are animals in more ways than most of us care to recognize. But we are also human, and I believe being human means we are the ones in the animal kingdom who are most capable of learning, growing, and changing our behavior for the better.

There are times during which we want to remain ignorant of abuse. It is in our nature to wish for things to stay as they are. But in order to survive abuse, we must become aware; we must learn about ourselves, grow, and change for the better. Speaking up, or listening when someone else speaks up, is the first and most important part of helping and respecting each other. And it's often the hardest part.

What I hope to accomplish with this book series is to give readers the idea that abuse or "bullying" is all around us, and it is a part of life. Still, its being part of life does not mean it has to continue. My story, sad as it is, I believe is still one of hope; of standing up from within despair and grabbing hold of the hand which is held out to you. Help and hope will come. Watch for them and in the meantime, protect yourself and those you know.

————————

John Emil Augustine is an author at Master Koda Select Publishing. He toured in his twenties and early thirties with local and national acts; writing, arranging, and performing on the road with well-known Jazz, Blues, Gospel, Reggae, Post Funk, Prog Rock, and Folk Rock groups. John has also been a landscaper, mail carrier, English professor, and forklift operator. He currently lives in Minneapolis, MN with his wife and four boys.

Learn more about him by visiting these websites: http://masterkodaselectpublishing.com and http://www.johnemilaugustine.com

Anti-Bully: A World Without Bullying

Fran Lewis

Living in the real world you know that there are many people who enjoy tormenting others just for the sake of being mean. Some prey on those that are smaller or weaker in strength and hoping they can demean them or make them feel worthless. Others might belittle someone for the way they dress, talk, or even walk down the street. These cruelties are not just distinctive of teens or young kids; adults are guilty too. In a world where violence seems to reign on the news, wars are front page, and hate crimes make you wonder what this world has become, bullying rears its ugly head in each of these cases. Whether it's a brawl in a public place, a fight in the schoolyard, or an argument over a parking space, no matter how you turn it one person is trying to strong arm another, and if the term fits use it.

Reading a newspaper or watching the news, it's not uncommon to hear about suicides related to teens being harassed online or in school. It is not uncommon to hear that the behaviors of your youth have become so bent in some cases, not all on hurting others that appear to be weaker, disabled in some respect or just not as physically able to defend themselves leaving them prey to gangs, attacks in the locker room and or verbal abuse. Many schools have prevention programs and some intervention programs, but just how successful are these and why can't we stop it from happening?

My name is Bertha and I am a teen that would love to create a world without wars, fighting, hate, and bullying. But, I am not sure that will ever happen because violence seems to riddle our streets in most neighborhoods whether affluent or not. Walking in the lunchroom the other day I heard some kids talking about hurting poor Nat because he deserved it. Why?

They disliked the way he talked, and because he was a "nerd" and really smart, he deserved to be punished. Anyone that does not conform to their gang mentality or belong in their group they feel does not deserve to breathe the same air as they do, even if you might say the air they breathe is tainted!

What would a world without bullying look like? Picture this: no physical, verbal, or non-verbal threats. Imagine using the net for research, Facebooking your friends, homework, downloading novels and not using your computer to bully someone else to the point they might commit suicide. Each form of bullying is hurtful and the person or persons delivering the abuse never show signs of remorse, nor do they care about the end result. Wonder how they would feel if they were at the receiving end? It might be a great way to teach them a lesson in the long run if they are ever finally stopped. How about a bully lesson for the person bullying so they can see how it feels? Maybe they will understand if this is done in a professional setting. Verbal abuse is what I was a victim of when people would say I was fat, ugly, and had a big nose. At times they said I dressed like a huge polka dot and looked like a beached whale. I never let on that I was hurt and the ability to lose weight, which I did, stopped the fat jokes, and changing how I dressed was not because of what they said… it was my choice. You own who you are, not them. Sometimes walking in the halls the mean girls or the popular ones would stare down other girls and hope they would start to cry. They would say nothing, but you got the point. Sometimes they would pretend to talk about you, laugh when you walked by, and point fingers at you. The trick was to pretend you didn't see it and not let on that they got to you. Harder than you might think! Harsh words, curse words, bumping into you in the hall, writing nasty words on your locker are just part of what they are capable of doing. Imagine a world where everyone said good morning. People complimented you on how you looked and others tried to help you look better. Imagine a world with no bullying.

Walk in the halls, down the street and do not ignore what might be happening right in front of you. If you see someone in trouble do not just stand there, do something. Bullies feel empowered when they have the support of others like them. If you or a friend are faced with this situation you can do a lot to help yourself or the person being bullied: You can talk to the person and make sure they are not hurt or if they need help. Find an adult to help, and even tell the bully to get away from the person and leave them alone. Students trained in peer mediation in a school with this type of intervention program are most helpful. Find a teacher, principal, or guidance counselor. Call the office for help on your cell phone. The bully does not need to know you are the one who reported them.

From the violence of video games to the programs on television that most kids watch we all need to work together to stop what so many have put in place. There are tons of resources out there. Some states have anti-bullying laws. All schools should have programs that are in place and teachers, parents and even students should understand they are mandate to report it. Schools have to do more to make it safe for kids to go to school. Guards have to assist teachers when things get out of hand. Posters, kids working together, community leaders, thinking positively and teaching kids how to interact in a positive way are just some ways we might actually succeed in creating a world where kids and adults get along.

Close your eyes and listen: No one is fighting. No one is yelling. No one is screaming. The games kids play, the music they listen to, and the friends they keep: wouldn't it be nice if everyone got along doing these same things we used to do as kids? Bullying: Let's try to make it a thing of the past and not the present. My name is Bertha and I have formed a peer intervention group in my school along with my sister Tillie. Read *Bertha and Tillie Sisters Forever: Bertha Fights Back* to find out just how I did it!

HATOCRACY

DJ Swerdloff

Tuesday, September 24, 2013: California lawmakers move to shield illegal immigrants from deportation

Immigration advocates are trying to get a proposed bill titled the *"Trust Act"* signed into law by Governor Jerry Brown after it passed the state Senate by a vote of 24 to 10. The Trust Act would make it more difficult for California police officers to assist federal officials in the deportation of illegal immigrants because it would "prohibit local jailers from holding most arrestees for an additional forty-eight hours before federal authorities arrive." The cases where they could be detained the additional forty-eight hours while federal officials arrive are crimes considered serious like child abuse, burglary, and murder. Under this bill, crimes like selling illegal drugs in small quantities would be considered minor because it would be a misdemeanor and those same drug dealers can go out and continue to sell because they can't be held long enough for anything to be done.

This proposed bill is causing much debate because it limits the abilities of police officers to do their job and because The California State Sheriffs' Association believes that local officials should leave immigration to federal officials, which involves holding those arrested until federal officials arrive. Debate is also occurring because the bill is seen as unconstitutional. The debate over it being unconstitutional is occurring due to the fact that the proposed bill would allow the state to restrict the ability of the federal government to enforce immigration law stated in federal code 8 1373(a).

In my honest opinion this bill shouldn't even be up for discussion, because the fact that they are here *illegally* should be the only argument officers need to be able to hold those arrested forty-eight hours while federal officials arrive. Section 274 of the Federal Immigration and Nationality Act makes it a federal felony to be in this country illegally, and last time I checked a felony is a serious crime. Then there is the Supreme Court ruling in the case of *The United States v. Verdugo-Urquidez* in which they ruled that "the people" protected by the Amendments to the Constitution "refers to a class of persons who are part of a national community or who have otherwise developed sufficient connection with this country to be considered part of that community." Meaning that even if the Trust Act passes, bail could be set so high for illegal immigrants that there is no way they can pay it because they aren't protected by the eighth amendment, which protects against excessive fines and excessive bail, making the bill useless. In conclusion, this proposed bill would restrict the ability of police officers to do their job, is dangerous because it allows for the release of dangerous criminals captured on a lesser charge, and is unconstitutional, yet people still think Governor Jerry Brown should sign it into law.

SURGERY

What Questions to Ask Before Saying Yes!

Fran Lewis

"You are going to need or require surgery. You have no choice. The procedure needs to be done and as soon as possible." Imagine hearing those words, having to process them, and hopefully begin comprehending all that those simple words in three short sentences entailed. Facing surgery and wondering why I needed to undergo it was only part of the story the reasons behind it quite upsetting. Imagine going for a routine comprehensive dental exam to find out that within your left mandible jaw there was something as the dentist described it called an *"entity,"* living within your lower left jaw. Listening to what the dentist stated and suggesting I call my oral surgeon took some time to process, but I did. With my trusty cell phone in my hand I called for an appointment that day. One painful biopsy later and one week of waiting for the results yielded the answers.

Listening to the oral surgeon relate that I had a cyst in my jaw that had to have been there for quite some time was more than upsetting, since I had been seeing another dentist for extensive procedures for quite some time. However, although full sets of films of my mouth were taken, nothing was ever said about this growth by anyone in his office. So, now I had to face surgery and I had a ton of questions to ask and get answered. Sharing my experience with readers is one thing, but helping you understand the questions you need to ask before undergoing any surgery is my goal. I hope that my personal questions that I asked both the surgeon and the anesthesiologist will help guide you when deciding whether to have surgery or not.

Most doctors welcome your questions and want to alleviate your fears and worries before undergoing any procedure. Asking these questions and having them explained is important. If there is anything that you do not understand you need to ask your physician to explain more clearly. Never speak with any surgeon or doctor without a family member or friend to take notes and hear what is being said. More than one set of ears is vital and you, as the patient might be so nervous you might not process, understand or remember everything that is being said. Here are the questions that I must have asked more than must once:

- Why is this procedure or operation necessary?
- What type of surgery are you recommending?
- What if I do not want the procedure? Are there any other options?
- What is the cost and is it covered by my insurance company and if so which one or ones?
- What out of pocket expenses can I expect?
- What are the risks and benefits of this surgery?
- What are the more serious risks?
- What are some things that can go wrong?
- What should I expect after surgery?
- How long is the recovery period?

- In my case: What am I allowed to eat or not eat?

- Where can I get a second opinion?

- Where is the surgery or procedure being performed? Why in this type of facility?

- What type of anesthesia will I need? Will it make me nauseas; sick or tired when I wake up?

- How long is the recovery period?

Making sure that your surgery is safe is vital so the following questions are important: I also asked who the anesthesiologist was that was going to do the surgery, and I did receive a call from the head anesthesiologist of the surgical center to discuss the various types of anesthesia and how they would be administered.

These questions should be asked of all the doctors that will be part of your surgical team: these need to asked before you decide which surgeon, where, when and why:

If you do have a choice of surgeon or hospital ask:

- What are your qualifications?

- Are you board certified and in what field?

- Are you certified in the field related to my specific surgery?

- Where can I learn about you and see your credentials? (I did the research before making the phone call to decide on my oral surgeon. I conferred with a well-known oral surgeon making sure that I chose the right person to perform the procedure. Asking this other oral surgeon to confer over the phone and discuss my options played a vital part in making many decisions and understanding what the procedure entailed.

- How much experience do you have doing this operation? How many have you done?

- Where will it be done? At which hospital or surgical center?

- How long do I have to remain in the hospital or surgical center after the surgery is completed? Have the surgeon explain and mark the site where the surgery will take place so that you know where on your body this will be performed.

- What are the benefits of having this done? What are the cons of not having it done?

- What can I expect after the operation: Pain, recovery period and what type of medications will I need?

When I met the anesthesiologist right before the surgery I asked him so many questions I thought he would stay to administer the anesthesia. I was more nervous about being put to sleep than what the operation entailed which was difficult enough:

Questions I asked:

- What type of anesthesia: Local, regional or general: Explain all of them

- What can I expect during recovery and in the recovery room when I wake up?

- Will I feel sick, tired or plain awful?

- What are the hospital and surgeon fees? Are they all in one or separate?

Make sure that you inform your primary doctor that you are having surgery and get medical clearance before the procedure is performed. Make sure the surgical team and your surgeon has a copy of this form and the results.

Asking for a second or third opinion is the way to ensure that you should have the procedure and there is no other decision that can be made.

Medicare may pay for a second opinion but in some cases more than one consultation might not be covered but it is worth the second and third opinion even if it is just for your own peace of mind.

Surgery is not always the answer but in my case it was the only one. The cyst was found on October 1,

2013 and was removed October 30. As of right now I am numb on the left side of my chin, lower jaw, the inside of my mouth is numb, and I cannot feel my teeth or whatever they did not remove. I lost three teeth that were wrapped around this huge cyst, and the feeling in my lower jaw both inside and out. My lower lip on the left side is numb and so is the inner lip. There are times I feel like someone is sitting on my face, lip, and chin pressing against it. But, it could have been worse and I might have lost feeling in my entire mouth, lip, and both sides of my jaw. Hopefully, I will get the feeling back, but for right now I am still eating soft foods, nothing hard like pizza crust, bagels, hard rolls, hard fruit or hard candy. I try and puree everything and have to even make sure that I eat on one side of my mouth because I cannot really tell or feel hot or cold on the left side.

These are the questions that I hope you will ask before undergoing surgery. Am I sorry that I had the operation? No: It saved my life, my jaw from fracturing, and it was the right decision and with the right surgical team. — 1/22/14

BRAND NEW DAY

Janet Yarkowsky isn't a real person, nor is she based on anyone I know. Her story came to me in dreams over a series of nights—strange for someone who never remembers her dreams. I felt compelled to sort through the words and images given to me and I hope I have written a true and cohesive version of the story. This story really touched my heart. I hope it will also touch yours. ~ Dellani

CONTINUED FROM LAST ISSUE

CHAPTER 3

Diego met the girls at the bus loop again, giving them a hand as they stepped off.

"I'm rethinking my car pool buddies," he said as Janet lost her balance and fell into his arms. "Yup. You girls are a lot prettier than the bozo twins." He jerked his head at Raul and their friend Tony.

"You'd throw me over for a chick?" Raul asked.

"In a heartbeat," Diego replied.

Raul laughed, tapping his friend's knuckles. "I feel ya, my brother. If you decide to throw us out, let me know. I'll find another ride, no biggie."

"What about me?" Tony asked.

"I'll find you a ride too," Raul said. "Whiner."

"Wienie."

Diego walked Janet to her first class. His own was just down the hall. Again, he felt the urge to kiss her, but public displays were against the rules and he could get himself thrown off the swim team if he broke that serious a rule. He talked himself into moving slowly.

"See you at lunch?"

"See you." Her dark eyes glittered with happiness.

***

Janet watched him walk down the hall, admiring the way he moved. His snug jeans clung to every muscle in his legs, making the view a very tasty one. She was almost late getting to her seat, scooting in as the bell rang.

Mr. Whitmore looked up expectantly as she clattered into her seat. "Did I miss something? Fire drill or something?"

"No, sir."

"You okay, Janet?"

"Yes, sir. Sorry. I was talking to someone...."

He nodded. "I won't dock you this time. Next time, cut it short."

She blushed, mumbling compliance. He flashed a grin at her. "As long as you're in the room before the bell, I'm not gonna fuss. Just be more careful, please. I don't want you to break your neck trying to sit down."

The time until lunch seemed interminable. Janet couldn't believe how much she looked forward to seeing Diego. When she walked to the table, he scooted aside, inviting her to sit next to him. Janet wasn't sure what he was doing, but she sat next to him—not too close. He scooted closer, his thigh and shoulder brushing hers. A little thrill ran through her when he smiled down at her.

"You ever have one of their cinnamon rolls?"

Janet shook her head. She always brought her lunch.

"Man, you need to try one."

He hopped up and bought her a hot, gooey treat, cutting line to do it. No one complained. Diego was captain of every team he was on, plus he had the well earned reputation of being able to kick the ass of anyone who crossed him. He paid for the cinnamon roll and carried it back to the table. Breaking off a piece, he put it to her lips.

"Try it." He teased her lips apart with the sweet bread.

Janet took the proffered bite, closing her eyes as the caramel topping melted in her mouth and the burst of cinnamon tickled her tongue.

"Oh, that's so good! Thank you."

He handed her the plate. "They're fantastic. Here. I all ready ate one. I don't need two. Trying to keep in shape." He patted his firm, flat abdomen.

"Thanks." Janet blushed, ducking her head as she accepted his gift.

She ate the roll after she finished her sandwich. It was one of the best tasting things she'd ever eaten, and she swore she'd learn how to make them just for Diego.

Trina walked her to class again. They stopped by the auditorium which was right by the drama room.

"So, are you and Diego dating?"

Janet shrugged, shaking her head. "He asked me to a movie Saturday. It's not like a date or anything...."

Trina smirked, her dark green eyes twinkling. "Yeah, right, sugar. And the Pope's Jewish."

Janet blinked and her mouth dropped open. Trina walked away, waving. Again, Janet was almost late for class, sliding in the door just as Mrs. Frost came over to close it.

"Sorry," she said as she neatly avoided a collision with the petite, blonde haired woman.

"What's with you today?" One of her classmates from Mr. Whitmore's class asked her. "That's twice in one day."

"I've got to learn when to shut up," she said, folding her hands in front of her.

The boy nodded, grinning. He'd seen her at lunch with Diego. After class, he walked with her, stopping at the chorus room.

"So, you dating Diego?"

"Scotty, no. I mean, we're going out Saturday...."

He nodded, a knowing smile on his lips. "Well, good luck with that."

"What's wrong with everyone today? Diego asked me to a movie. It's not a date!"

"Um, I'm pretty sure *he* thinks it's a date."

Janet didn't have a chance to talk to Diego until after school. He walked her to her locker, offering her a ride home with him, Ramona, and Bunny.

"I'd love one. I hate riding the bus."

"Cool. I need to stop at my locker. I'll meet you back here in a few minutes."

"I'll be here. I have to wait for Ramona and Bunny anyway."

"Okay. See you." He grinned, blowing her a kiss.

Janet blushed when people in the hall whistled and cheered. She got her things from her locker as she waited for her friends.

"Where were you?" Janet asked when they walked up.

"Giving you time to talk to Diego," Bunny replied. "He looked intent upon getting you alone."

"Oh, you guys are crazy. It's not like that."

"No? Okay." Bunny grinned, tossing her hair. She raised an eyebrow.

Diego rushed up moments later. "Ready to go?"

"Baby, I was born ready," Bunny said, winking saucily at him.

Diego laughed. "Great, a comedian." He put his arm around Janet's shoulders, but not around Bunny's as he often did.

They walked to the parking lot and spotted Diego's car. It was a white Barracuda with dark blue stripes on the hood and roof. He and his father were gradually rebuilding it. Ramona and Bunny got in the back, leaving Janet up front with Diego.

The powerful motor roared to life and he headed to Bunny's house. She clamored out of the back seat and waved as they pulled out of her driveway.

"Need to go by the store?" Diego asked Janet.

"No. Probably tomorrow, but we're good until then."

"Okay. Anytime you need to stop, tell me. It's not a big deal."

"Thanks."

"What are friends for?" He flashed his winning smile at her, dark eyes sparkling.

He stopped the car in her driveway, turning it off. He was trying to find some excuse either to get in the house or get his sister out of the car, but he couldn't think of a thing. Ramona solved the problem.

"Janet, I need to pee."

"Oh, sure. Come on." She hopped out and unlocked the door. "Coming?" she asked Diego.

He followed quickly.

Ramona smiled, winking at him as she shut the bathroom door. Diego took a step toward Janet.

"I'm really looking forward to Saturday," he said, taking her hand.

"Me too."

"Our first official date," he continued, taking another step.

Janet faltered, unsure how to respond. He saw the confusion in her eyes.

"Is there a problem?"

"No. No, I didn't think it was a *date*-date."

"What did you think it was?" He took another step. He was now about six inches from her.

Janet's heart pounded in her chest and she felt a little dizzy. Any second, Sookie would be home. She was confused by Diego's attention.

"I really like you, Janet. It took me forever to figure it out. But, I'd like to be your boyfriend."

"I'd—I'd like that too," she stammered, hardly able to meet his intense gaze.

"And I'd really like to kiss you," he continued, taking both her hands.

Not waiting for an answer, he pulled her close, taking her waist as he lowered his mouth to hers. Janet wasn't sure what to do. She closed her eyes and raised her chin.

Diego smiled. He knew she was inexperienced, but it didn't matter. He loved her and he'd teach her everything she needed to know. His lips touched hers, sending a spark from his lips to hers. Janet jumped back with a little *eep* of surprise. Laughing, he tugged her close once more.

"Sorry. Static." He tried again, this time without the power surge.

***

Janet didn't know what to expect, but it wasn't this. His lips were warm, full, soft, and tantalizing. It wasn't a long kiss, but it left her wanting more.

Diego held Janet around the waist, his lips barely touching hers. He kissed her twice more before letting go. Taking a step back, he opened his eyes. Janet lowered her chin, licking her lips as she opened her eyes too.

"I'll be by around seven-thirty, is that a good time?" Diego said self-consciously.

"Yes. Perfect. Thanks."

"What are boyfriends for?"

Janet squeaked excitedly, indulging in a bounce. Biting her lower lip, she tried to stop a giggle, but couldn't. About that time, she saw Ramona standing in the hallway. Her friend rushed her, taking her hands. They squealed, hopping a little in their excitement.

"Why do girls do that? Seriously? You're like little kids," Diego fussed.

"We're happy," Ramona said. "Deal with it, big brother."

Diego laughed loudly. "Sure. If it means I get another kiss."

"I'm gonna go wait in the car," Ramona said with a sly grin. "I'll honk when Sookie arrives."

Her brother and friend weren't fully listening. He was all ready taking advantage of the fact his sister was leaving. Before kissing Janet again, he pulled her close.

"Try something for me," he whispered.

"What?"

"Open your mouth—just a little."

Puzzled, she nodded. She closed her eyes, opening her mouth a bit. His tongue flickering into her mouth shocked her. She tried to pull away, but he held her close, kissing her much more emphatically. After the initial surprise, she relaxed against him, experimentally slipping her tongue into his mouth.

The horn honked outside, and Diego let her go. Sookie had arrived. If she caught them kissing, Janet would hear about it the rest of her life. She combed her fingers through her hair and dashed to the kitchen. She poured Diego a glass of water, handing it to him. Very loudly, he thanked her as Sookie slammed the front door.

"I'll see you in the morning," Diego said as he walked out of the narrow kitchen.

"Yeah. Thanks for the ride."

"Thanks for the water. Dang hiccups." He forced a burp, striking his chest with his fist. His dark eyes twinkled and he winked at Janet when Sookie wasn't looking.

Janet walked him to the door. He knew he didn't dare kiss her again, but he squeezed her fingers as he headed out the door.

"What's for supper?" Sookie asked.

"Leftovers."

Sookie turned up her nose, stalking to her room. She was a picky eater and hated leftovers. However, the food budget made that necessary. Janet paid for her own clothing, she refused to spend the rest of her money on food. She had a little savings account that she added to every week. It wasn't much, but it was her escape fund. As soon as she graduated, she was leaving. She could handle three more years of her mother and Sookie, but that was her limit.

About an hour later, the phone rang. Janet was just finishing her homework. Sookie got to the phone before she did.

"Who's this?" Sookie said when she answered.

"We don't answer the phone like that," Janet reprimanded.

"It's for you," Sookie said, handing her the phone.

"Who is it?"

"Some boy." She shrugged.

Janet took the phone, sitting at the kitchen counter. Sookie wandered into her room, but Janet suspected she was eavesdropping.

"Hello?"

"Hey, it's me," Diego said. "Sookie's got a real phone presence."

"I know. She could work for the phone company."

There was a longish pause. Janet thought maybe he'd hung up.

"Hello?"

"I'm here. Sorry. I thought maybe you'd keep talking." He laughed at himself. "I didn't really call with a reason—except I wanted to hear your voice. That makes me sound like an idiot. Forget I said that."

"No, it's sweet. Thank you. Do you really want to be my boyfriend?" she said very quietly.

"Yeah, of course I do. I wouldn't have asked you otherwise. I really like you, Janet. I didn't realize until yesterday just how much."

"I like you too," she said softly. "More than I ever thought."

"I'm glad, cause I'd feel like a real goob if you didn't."

"You're still a goob," Janet teased.

"Oh, thanks!" He laughed.

Janet heard a muffled man's voice in the background.

"Dammit, sorry. My brother needs the phone. I'll see you in the morning."

"Bye, Diego."

"Bye, Janet."

***

He wanted badly to tell her he loved her, but that wouldn't be his best move. Instead, he hung up and gave the phone to his brother.

Carlos apologized. "I forgot to call my girl today. I heard you talking to Janet and remembered. She's gonna be freaking."

"No, it's okay. So, a new girl, huh?" He punched Carlos as he dialed the phone.

"Ow! Yeah, she's pretty cool. You'd like her. I think I'm gonna.... Hey, baby. It's me...."

Diego wandered outside. His father sat on the front porch smoking a cigarette.

"So, you and Janet, huh?" He smiled, nodding. "I'm proud of you, son."

"Really? What for?"

"For making a commitment."

"We're just dating, Dad. We're not getting married."

His father chuckled. "I know. But this is the one. This is the girl you'll end up with."

"I hope so. She's really special to me."

His father clapped him on the back. "You need to head to bed, son. It's getting late."

Diego nodded. "Night, Dad."

His father nodded and smiled, taking a long drag on his cigarette.

***

Janet sat by the phone a long time before deciding to go to bed. When she lay down, she could feel Diego's lips on hers, caressing them. The touch of his hands sent thrills down her spine, making her shiver with delight.

Her dreams were highly erotic, though vague. She knew the mechanics of sex, but nothing more than she'd learned in health class. She was aware of the need for birth control and that the girl was supposed to keep saying no until she was married, but she also knew she had no intention of saying no forever. She cared about Diego and he made her feel special. His tender kisses warmed her heart, filling in the cold, empty places that riddled it when her father left.

"If he wants to.... If he asks me, I'm not gonna say no."

***

The next morning, Ramona and Diego arrived at 7:30 as planned. They picked up Bunny and headed to school. Diego gave Janet a quick kiss before they went into the building and he walked her to class, holding her hand.

At lunch, they sat together with their friends around them. In their own little world, they hardly noticed anyone else. Trina burst into their private bubble.

"So, are you two officially dating now?" She leaned forward, arms on the table.

Diego laughed. "Yes, Trina. We're a couple. Got a problem with that?"

"Not at all, I was just dying to know. I'm glad to have that decided. Now I can quit wondering and get on with my life." She tossed her hair, catching Raul in the face.

He laughed, spitting her hair out. "Baby, if you want my attention, there's other things you can do."

"I thought you needed a mouthful, babe. Sorry."

He laughed louder, leaning over to nibble on her neck. He mumbled something that Janet didn't hear. Trina elbowed his ribs, blushing.

"Ready for class?" she asked Janet.

"Yeah." Janet hopped up.

Diego joined them. "I'll head that way."

"Okay, we'll let you," Trina said with a sly grin.

She left them behind, heading into the auditorium. Diego caught the door, slipping in after her, dragging Janet with him. He pulled the door shut behind them, surprising her with a kiss.

"I've been dying to do that all day. I can't stay long or I'm gonna be late." He took one more quick kiss before pulling her back into the hallway.

Laughing, Janet jogged to her class. Diego took off at a dead run for his. She had the feeling he was going to be very late, but she knew he didn't care. They met up in chorus and she asked him.

"I was, but no big deal. It's not like I'm gonna flunk if I'm late. We'll just have to leave lunch a little earlier Monday so I can get my fix."

"You make it sound like a drug."

"Better than a drug, and I'm totally addicted."

He wouldn't kiss her in front of all these people, but Janet knew that he wanted too. They would have to wait.

After school, Bunny and Ramona told Diego they intended to ride with Betty to Bunny's house.

"You sure? Cause I can drop you."

"No, Janet needs to go by the store. We'll head to Bunny's…she's going to show me her new terrarium."

Diego frowned, pursing his lips. "Okay…. What's that?"

"It's for plants," Bunny replied.

"If you're sure."

"See you later, big brother." Ramona waved to Janet.

"They set us up," Janet said, laughing. "That was sweet."

"I don't know if I should be grateful or very, very afraid," Diego said as they walked to his car with their arms around one another. "Did you need to go to the store?"

"No. It can wait until Sunday."

"Cool…." He drove rapidly to her house and pulled up in the driveway.

"Want a cold drink?"

He nodded, grinning. "No. But I do want to come in."

"Okay."

The second the door was closed behind them, he kissed her. Cupping her face in his hands, he teased her lips apart, probing her mouth gently but adamantly. Somewhat taken aback by the strength of his desire, she took a step away from him.

"I'm sorry," he said. "I didn't mean to scare you. I know you're not experienced. I know you're not ready…. But I really—am being an asshole. I'm sorry." He stepped away from her.

"I'm not experienced. And I'm not ready *yet*…. But I will be, and when I am, I want it to be you." She took his face in her hands, pulling him to her.

He laughingly complied. "God, I love you, Janet. I've loved you since we were kids. Only I never thought…."

"I know," she whispered. "Me too."

They kissed until they heard a car pull up. It was Mrs. Thompson dropping off Sookie. Instead of just letting her out, she came up to the house with her. Janet dashed to the door, opening it wide.

"Hi, is there a problem?"

"No, it's fine. It's just I'm not sure that Lonnie's going to be in school on Monday. He's not feeling too well. I picked him up at noon."

"Thanks so much for getting Sookie anyway. That was really nice of you."

Mrs. Thompson ruffled Sookie's hair. "Can't leave my best travel buddy stranded."

"If there's ever a problem, please call me at school. I can make arrangements."

"Sweetie, it'll be a cold day in hell when I can't do a favor for a neighbor. Your mom works wicked hours and you can't drive yet. I don't mind. I know you'd do the same for me."

"I sure would. If you ever need to drop Lonnie here after school, let me know."

"Thanks, honey. I'll let your mom know about Monday. You might have to pick her up if your mom can't make other arrangements."

"Okay. Thanks."

"You gonna introduce me to your young man?"

Janet blushed. "I'm sorry. I thought you knew each other. This is my boyfriend, Diego Hernandez. This is my neighbor, Mrs. Thompson."

"Nice to meet you," they said in chorus, shaking hands.

"I hope Lonnie feels better soon," Janet said.

CHAPTER 4

Janet closed the door, leaning against it. "God, I hope she doesn't get sick. I'm the one who has to stay with her if she does. Mom can't take the time off."

"We'll figure out something. I bet Mom would watch her."

"I can't ask your mother to do that for me...."

"Yeah, you can. You've been Mona's friend forever. And you're the woman I—"

"Shh," Janet cautioned. "Little ears," she whispered.

"Sorry," he replied just as quietly. "Don't forget. Tomorrow."

"I can't forget something that special. Our first real date."

He gave her a last kiss before leaving. "I'll call later."

"How late can you stay out?" she asked abruptly.

"Tonight? Eleven."

"Me too. Want to come by after the Hell Spawn goes to bed?"

"I shouldn't...."

"Why not?" She couldn't hide her disappointment.

"'Cause, nighttime, a nearly empty house, beds...I'm gonna get all the wrong ideas," he whispered, tracing the line of her breast with one fingertip.

Janet swallowed her disappointment. "I didn't think of that. Sorry."

"No, I am. I'm a guy, that's how we think. I'm so hot for you I can hardly stand it. I'd turn into a cave-man and fornicate your brains out." Diego nipped her lower lip.

"I'd just keep telling you no." Janet tried to play tough, knowing it was an act.

"Only so long that works. When the primal takes over, that's it. I'm unstoppable—and you won't want to stop me anyway."

"Sure of your charms." She shoved him playfully away.

Diego took a step back, grinning. "You have no idea. Some women have found me particularly charming."

"How many women?" She withdrew slightly, pouting.

He blinked. "Mona asked me that too. What's the deal? So I've dated a few girls, got some experience. Is that a crime?"

"No. It's just that girls talk, D. They talk a lot."

"Ten," he said quietly. "Only ten. I've dated more than that, but I swear, I haven't been to bed with them all."

"That seems like a lot," she said, rather hurt by his honesty.

"That's only five girls a year," he complained. "That's not that many."

"I suppose not." She still wasn't convinced.

"Do we have to argue about this?"

She shook her head.

"Good, cause I don't want to argue. I do need to get going," he said. He gave her one last, quick kiss.

"Carlos is visiting. I promised to spend some time with him."

"Tell him I said hi."

"I'll do that." He kissed her hand and left.

She closed the door behind him with a sigh.

"Are you dating him now?" Sookie asked loudly from the hallway.

"What if I am?"

"Does Mom know?"

Janet didn't answer.

"I bet she doesn't. I bet she has no clue he's kissing you in the living room."

"Were you spying on me? You little…."

"You gonna have sex with him?"

"Sookie Ann! How dare you? He's my boyfriend. That doesn't automatically mean—and how do you know about that anyway? You're ten!"

"I'm not stupid. I do watch soap operas." Sookie rolled her eyes.

"I'm not talking to you. Do your homework." Janet headed to the kitchen.

Sookie followed her like a pestering little dog. "I'm telling Mom that he kissed you."

"Go ahead. He's my boyfriend, he has the right to kiss me." She didn't stop what she was doing, her back to her little sister.

"He's Ramona's brother…does *she* know?" She was trying every tactic she could to get under Janet's skin.

"Mona knows all about it. She's thrilled."

"But Mom doesn't know. I think I'll tell her. I bet she'd be real interested."

"Go ahead," Janet replied. "And I'll tell her who really broke into the shed and stole her bike. Then, maybe I'll tell her you take money from her purse all the time so you can by a soda at the corner store. And maybe I'll tell her about the time you—"

"You wouldn't! You can't!" Sookie stamped her foot.

Janet turned on her slowly, calmly. "Maybe it's time Mom knew that you aren't the perfect little girl she thinks you are. Perhaps I should enlighten her."

"She won't believe you! She'll believe me."

Janet smiled secretively. "Oh, she'll believe me, squirt. I can be very persuasive."

"You can't! She won't!"

Janet shrugged, going back to her work.

"I hate you! You're the meanest sister ever!" Sookie balled up her fist to hit Janet in the back.

Janet saw her sister in the window over the sink. She turned around in a flash, leaning menacingly toward her.

"Go ahead, half pint. Hit me. I dare you. I won't get you back right away, you misspent, addle brained, pipsqueak…." Janet lowered her voice an octave, dropping into a harsh, croaking whisper. "But you have to sleep sometime." She did an evil laugh.

Sookie screamed and ran to her room, slamming the door. Janet heard her lock it and pull a piece of furniture across the door. Janet continued to laugh, enjoying the feeling of power she had over her little sister. Of course, she might pay for it later, but for now, she held all the cards.

Janet planned to tell her mother about Diego after dinner. She fixed a roast chicken and all the side dishes her mother liked best. She even baked fresh cornbread, because her mother loved it.

When Ilene Yarkowsky walked in the house, she actually smiled. "It smells wonderful in this house! What's the occasion?"

"Do we need one to have a nice meal? I got the chicken on sale, so I thought we'd have roast tonight, then use the rest for chicken and dumplings tomorrow. What you think?"

"Oh, good idea. And boil down the bones for broth."

"Of course! Learned that from you and Nana. Don't waste a lick!" she said, just like her grandmother.

113

Her mother smiled again, hugging her for the first time in ages. "That's my mom! Did you make cornbread?" she asked as the timer dinged. "I'll get it." She took the cast iron skillet from the oven, inhaling deeply. "You trying to soften me up?" she asked warily.

"No, what a thing to say. It's a little celebration. End of the first week. And I got a place on the speech team doing a dramatic reading, and a solo in chorus."

"Really? How wonderful! You're gonna go far with that," her mother said, surprising her further. "Where's Sookie?"

"Hiding in her room."

"Hiding? Whatever for?"

"Who knows? Maybe she watched *Dark Shadows* again. Or *Psycho*. That shower scene scared the bejeezus outta me for weeks. I didn't even want to shower by myself downstairs." She laughed at her own silly fear.

"Well, serves her right then," Ilene said, wandering to her bedroom.

Janet knew that her mom would take off her uniform and have a shower before dinner. She set the cornbread on a rack to cool and checked the chicken. It looked perfect. Oven off, she stirred the butter beans and mashed the potatoes. She put plates in the oven to warm and made sure the table was set.

Her mother came out of the shower and changed into her house dress before coming to the table. Janet called Sookie and they sat down to dinner together. Her mother offered grace and they ate in silence a few minutes. When her mother seemed in the best frame of mind, Janet broached her final subject.

"I'm going to the movie on Saturday."

"Really? With Ramona?"

"Actually, I'm going with her brother. Diego asked me out."

"Diego. Asked you out?"

"Yes, Mom. It's okay, isn't it? We've known them for ages."

Her mother didn't say anything. She didn't lose her temper or frown.

"You're sure this is what you want?"

Kind of a weird question.

"Yes, Mom. I really like him. He's the nicest boy I know and he's liked me a long time. He just didn't think it was appropriate to ask me out before I got in high school."

Her mother nodded. She said nothing for a long time.

"I think it's lovely," she said quietly. "Diego is a nice boy. He's very bright, focused. He'll go far."

"Yes, I think so too. This doesn't mean we're getting married or anything." Janet laughed casually.

"I think it's wonderful," her mother said with genuine warmth. "I'm happy for you."

"Thanks."

"Sookie, go clean up. Janet, I need some help with something in the storage room."

"Yes, ma'am." Janet cleared her dishes and they went to the basement.

The house was two levels, one above ground, one below. The basement had a bathroom, two bedrooms, the utility room, and a large, paneled family room. Janet had the larger basement bedroom. The second, smaller bedroom was the storage room. It was crammed full of boxes and bins that her mother moved around periodically, trying to organize, but it never came to much.

She walked in, shutting the door behind them, and sat on one of the boxes, indicating that Janet should sit too.

"I know you know about how your body works," she said calmly. "And you've learned about sex in school. But you don't know about boys, not really. This is your first real boyfriend. Are you sure this is what you want?"

"Mom, I really care about him so much!" She didn't dare say she loved him, her mother wouldn't believe her.

"A man only takes no for an answer so long," her mother continued. "And then he expects certain things."

Janet nodded, knowing where this was going. "I know, Mom. Diego won't force me into anything I'm not ready for."

"It's that I'm worried about," her mother said, touching her cheek tenderly. "He's a handsome boy, very sweet, but he's still a man. We're going to start you on birth control pills. I'll buy you condoms."

"Mama!" Janet was horrified.

"I'm not condoning this, I want that understood. And you'd better not ever do a thing in this house but kiss him." The stern mother was back, gaining power. "But I understand about being swept off your feet," her mother returned to the uncharacteristic calm. "Your father, despite his faults, was a handsome, desirable man, and he lit a fire in me that I haven't had before or since. He was my first," she mused. "And the best. I loved him so much...."

"Why did you leave him? I mean, I know.... But was *that* really all?"

"It wasn't because of his heritage," her mother said, stiffening. "He lied to me. For years, he lied."

"Was being married to—to a man like him, so awful?"

"It was the lie, Janet. The flat out lie that we lived. If he lied about that, what else had he lied about? Could I really trust him anymore?" She shrugged, tears falling.

"Would you have married him if you'd known at the time what he was?"

Her mother shrugged, shaking her head. "I don't know. But there's never been a man as loved me like Evander."

"But would you?"

Her mother smiled, tears running down her face. "In a heartbeat! You take that love you've got and hold on tight with both hands, Janet May. That boy loves you and you love him, I can see it when you say his name. But you take it slow and you make him work

hard to win you. Don't give up easy. And don't you sleep around. You stick with one man and your life will be a lot happier."

Janet nodded. This wasn't the conversation she'd expected from her mother. Mama was much more prone to hateful words and cold shoulders. While her mother was in this mellow mood, Janet asked a question that burned in her heart.

"Mama, why do you hate me so?"

Her mother burst into tears, grabbing her daughter in her arms. "Janet May, I don't hate you! I just look at you and I see your daddy and all I lost. I see the mean way I've been and I can't make it stop. I'm broke and I'm tired and I know if I'd stayed with your daddy, my life wouldn't be so harsh. But I made up my mind and I did what I did. I can't take it back."

"But what if you could? What if he'd take us back?"

Her mother smiled. "Can't live your life on *what if*, baby girl." Sniffing loudly, she wiped her eyes with her fingers.

Janet got some toilet paper from the tiny bathroom so Mama could wipe her eyes and blow her nose.

"Now, we need to find something to carry up so your sister won't have a snit wondering what we left her out of." She looked around and found an ugly Hawaiian doll that danced if you touched it. "Think she'd like that for her room?"

"That's the ugliest thing I've ever seen. She'll love it."

Laughing, they walked upstairs and presented Sookie with the doll. She took it to her room and stayed there all evening long.

***

Saturday, Janet got through her shift at the drive-in on automatic. Her mind was completely occupied with thoughts of Diego. Even thinking his name made her heart flutter. By the time her shift ended, she was anxious to see him.

At 3:02, she changed from her uniform into a new outfit. She slid on her new Levi's straight leg, button up jeans and pulled a lime green T-shirt over her head. She switched her work shoes for a pair of leather sandals and put on a pair of plastic hoops that matched her shirt. A quick brush up on her makeup, and she was ready.

Diego walked in just as she returned to the restaurant. He took her hands, smiling.

"Is it okay if I kiss you?"

She glanced at her boss. He didn't look like he was in a very lenient mood. There weren't any rules about kissing someone when she was off duty, but why make him mad? She shook her head slightly. They walked out to Diego's car. Before opening the door, he pressed his long, muscular body against hers, placing his hands on either side. The kiss, when it came, was nothing like any he'd given her before. It was full of desire, love, and animalistic power. It was frightening and titillating all at once.

Janet sighed, relaxing against the car as her hands went around his waist. He made a noise in his throat that sounded like a growl. Janet tried not to laugh, but she was nervous all ready. His behavior made her more so. The laughter bubbled out, forcing them apart. He gazed down at her with a slightly glazed expression.

"What?" He mumbled.

"What was that noise?"

"What noise?"

"That one you made just now?" She imitated it.

"I did that?" He laughed, putting his arm around her shoulders, as he flopped against the car. "I have no idea. Maybe I was purring."

She giggled, meeting his penetrating gaze. "Purring? Like a cat?"

"Why not? They purr when they're content. Why can't a man?"

"That's pretty weird, Diego."

He shrugged, chuckling. "Yeah, well.... You make me content, happy...."

He didn't add that she also filled him with lust unmatched by any other he'd ever felt. He wanted to be with her more than any other girl he'd dated. It wasn't that she was any prettier, or any sexier, it was that he loved her.

It took a moment for his mind to find its way back to the mundane. He'd been falling deeper into lust mode and had to climb out again. He hoped she didn't notice that his pants were suddenly extra tight across the front. He wished he'd worn loose fitting jeans. Mentally kicking himself, he opened her car door and helped her get settled.

They parked behind the theatre in the employee parking lot and walked around the front. The girl at the ticket counter didn't charge them for the tickets she gave them. They were able to walk right in and head to the concession stand for popcorn and drinks. The girl there charged only half price.

"Oh, the perks of dating a man who works at the movies," Janet murmured as they walked into the theatre.

"It's part of the job," he said. "Really, she should have charged me for your ticket, but we're buddies."

"Is she one of your old girlfriends?" Janet turned somewhat chilly.

Diego took her chin, turning her face to his. "No. She's a friend. We never dated. She's with a buddy of mine and has been for six years. Just so we're clear, I haven't dated anyone here. Feel better now?"

She smiled, kissing him playfully on the nose. "Yes."

"Good. Where do you want to sit?"

"I'll let you choose. You've been here more than me."

"Would you be willing to sit in the balcony?"

"Depends on where. I'm not good with heights."

"I won't let you fall," he promised, holding her close. "Balcony has the best view."

"Okay, I'll take your word for it."

They walked up to the balcony and he led her to a pair of seats about halfway up, in the center. Janet's head spun a little. She closed her eyes when she sat down.

"You okay?" Diego asked.

"Yeah. This will take a little getting used to."

"Maybe I can help." He set their food and drinks down.

Next thing she knew, he kissed her. The strength of his embrace made her forget everything else. Now, the dizziness was from desire, not fear. That dissipated too, leaving her feeling content.

The house lights came down and the cartoon started. They sat close, watching and laughing. The previews came next and Diego told her about things he wanted to see. He was a real movie buff, just like she was, and they had the same taste in movies.

"We'll see that when it comes out," he told her after each of them.

"I'd like that."

"Cool." He gave her a quick kiss.

The movie started. They watched for some time, munching popcorn and sipping their drinks. About thirty minutes in, Diego set his refreshments aside. He took Janet's, setting them down too. The theatre was dark, nearly deserted. There was only one other person in the balcony and he was asleep. It was as close to alone as they were likely to get.

Diego's eyes sparkled in the light from the movie as he moved closer. Janet wasn't quite sure what he wanted until he smiled and touched her cheek. Smiling back, she leaned toward him. His lips met hers, his fingers drifted from her cheek to her neck. He played with her hair, winding his fingers in it.

His kiss was electrifying. Janet felt a tingle from her lips spreading all over her body. It lodged low in her belly, waking feelings she'd never had before. She understood now what her mother meant. It would be awfully hard to tell him no if he wanted to take this further than just kissing. Her body betrayed her, giving in to his touch.

Soon, there was nothing on her mind but his lips on hers, his arm around her shoulders, his fingers in her hair. His left hand brushed her neck, making her shiver. It dropped to her shoulder and down. She felt the heat of his hand near her breast, not quite touching. The heat intensified as his fingers moved tantalizingly close to her chest. The touch of his hand scorched her with fear, desire, and embarrassment. She pushed away from him.

His lips followed her retreating mouth, desperately trying to recapture her. Opening his eyes, he realized what he was doing. His hand jumped away from her body and a guilty smile replaced the lust.

"Sorry," he whispered. "Went into caveman mode." He kissed her neck and nibbled on her earlobe by way of apology. His left hand stayed steadfastly in his own lap.

"When do you think I'll be ready?" Janet asked, bowing to his experience.

Diego chuckled. "Baby, I have no way of knowing that. That's different with every girl. When you feel like the time is right."

"What about you?"

He laughed loudly; fortunately, it was a funny part of the film. He put his arms across the back of her seat and the one to his left, tossing back his head.

"Janet, I'm a man. It's always right for me."

She looked so hurt, he stopped laughing. "I'm being an asshole. I'm sorry. This is all yours. You have to decide when it's time. I won't push. All you have to know is that I'm here, I'm ready, and I want you whenever you give me the word." He took her face in his hands. "Do me a favor, though. Don't make me wait too long or I might bust." His kiss was playful.

"How long do most girls wait?"

He shrugged, pulling her close so she could put her head on his shoulder.

"Some a week, some a couple. I've never been with—someone like you."

"A virgin?" She said the word rather harshly.

Diego flinched as if she'd hit him. "Yeah." He glanced at her, kissing her lightly on the nose before turning back to the screen.

"Why not?"

"I dunno. Never happened before. Tell you the truth, it scares me a little."

"I didn't think anything could scare you."

"I didn't think so either. I don't want to hurt you. That scares me."

She nodded, snuggling closer. "You won't hurt me," she replied confidently. "When we make love, it will be wonderful."

CONTRIBUTORS

Allan Topol, author

Allan is the national bestselling author of eight novels of international intrigue, including *Spy Dance.* His novels have been translated into Chinese, Japanese, Portuguese, and Hebrew. He is a graduate of Carnegie Institute of Technology, who majored in chemistry, abandoned science, and obtained a law degree from Yale University. A partner in a major Washington law firm, and an avid wine collector, he has traveled extensively, researching dramatic locations for his novels. You can join him on Facebook. Please let him know if you would like to receive his free newsletter. Allan is available for speaking opportunities on subjects of international affairs, dealt with in his novels.

Visit his website: www.allantopol.com

Ann Stanmore, author

Ann retired in 2007, having stayed on at work an extra couple of years. She had an interesting and busy job and now has an interesting and busy retirement. Writing is her main interest at the moment, and she is working on a sequel to her first book, *Well, It Was Fun.*

Barbara Watkins

Barbara Watkins resides in Missouri with her husband and loyal boxweiler, Hooch. In her writings, she loves to evoke a false sense of security and expectations, as she leads her reader into a world of the unknown. Her articles on various subjects, short stories, and poetry, have appeared in 2008 *New York Skyline Review,* and several on-line publications. *Cold Coffee Magazine* accepted her article, "A Testament To Poets," for their second issue released in print and is available online at Cold Coffee Magazine.

In 2010, Watkins collaborated with New Zealand director, Dimi Nakov, on a screenplay for a short movie titled "BlindSide." Her name appears at the film's end credits for voice-over monologue. "BlindSide" was accepted into the Cannes short film corner as part of the 65th Festival de Cannes as well as the 7th Cyprus International Film Festival 2012, and many more prestigious film festivals.

Many of her short stories and novella, *Thorns of an Innocent Soul,* have been optioned to New Zealand film production company, Zodiac Entertainment, for screenplay adaptation to film.

Previous Publications: *Mortal Abomination — Awaken Spirit — Hollowing Screams — Six-Pack of Blood* (co-author, Betty Dravis) *Six-Pack of Fear* (co-author, Betty Dravis). Anthologies include, *Hope Whispers* (compiled by Lynn C. Johnston) *Live Life: The Daydreamer's Journal* (compiled by Sir Ricky McGentleman) *Satan's Holiday,* an anthology of scary stories (compiled by Yvonne Mason) and *Writing Tips From Authors* (compiled by Patti Roberts.)

Visit her website: www.barbarawatkins.net

Brian Hayden, author

Brian Hayden was born in Chicago, Illinois, in 1954 into a middle-class, blue-collar, Jewish family. He is the middle child with a brother one year older senior, and a sister two years younger. In 1961, his family moved to the suburbs of Los Angeles, California. He is a second generation, American-born son of Austrian and English grandparents on his father's side, and Polish and Russian grandparents on his mother's side. He enlisted in the United States Air

Force in 1972, and was finally medically discharged in July of 1990.

He published his earliest book in 1999, titled *Using Strategic and Tactical Planning to Make Your Veterinary Practice More Profitable*. During that period, he wrote five scripts for educational videos. Then, in February of 2011, he published his memoir, *Death: Living To Talk About It*. On August 20, 2012, he published his first work of fiction, *Five Short Stories and Twelve Poems*. Now, after more than two years in the works, *Road To Transplant*, his sequel to the memoir was published in 2012. He continues to write both fiction and nonfiction and maintains a weekly blog.

Christoph Fischer, author

Christoph Fischer was born in Germany in 1970 but moved on to the UK in the early 1990s where he is still resident today. *The Luck of The Weissensteiners* is his first published work and concerns a Jewish Family in Slovakia during the 1930s and 1940s. *Sebastian* his second book about a young handicapped man in Vienna in the 1910s was published in May 2013. He has written several other novels, which are in the later stages of editing and finalization. Both of his book have received critical acclaim and have entered the indie tribe fiction charts and the Amazon charts for Jewish Fiction.

He is currently on of the Top 1% of reviewers on Goodreads and #1727 reviewer on Amazon.

His recommendations and reviews can be found at http://writerchristophfischer.wordpress.com/ and http://www.christophfischerbooks.com

David and Faith McDonald

David S. McDonald is a minister, along with his wife, Faith of Whole Heart Abundance ministries (W.H.A.M.,INC.) of Chattanooga, Tenn. They have two children Shane Isbill and Shannon Isbill also of Chattanooga and four grandchildren: Christian, Ashlyn, Jared, and Elise. David has widely read from many disciplines of life and study, incorporating these bodies of knowledge into the stories he writes. His writing influences also include such writers of fiction as Sir Arthur Conan Doyle, Isacc Asimov, Theodore Sturgeon, Ray Bradbury, Stephen King and many others. He is also a student of all religions and philosophies. Though, a devout Christian, David

takes an eclectic approach to world views, respecting all belief systems and the right of all to freely choose how they believe. Joy, faith, understanding, patience, love, forgiveness and integrity with God's strength lead him along his own path. He and his wife, Faith's heart's desire is to illuminate minds and heal hearts with the wisdom of peace, thereby, alleviating much of the World's suffering. Reason shall and must prevail.

David Workman, author

David Workman's debut novel, *Absolute Authority*, hit the shelves in early 2012 to roaring acclaim. A native St. Louisan, he was recently named by local television station KMOV as one of St. Louis' Top 5 New Authors. Along with writing novels, David has spent most of his 20-year writing career hammering out advertising and marketing copy for companies large and small, including his current gig as the lead contest specialist for a major athletic shoe company. His second novel, a sequel, is scheduled for a winter 2013 release. Find him on Facebook.

Dellani Oakes, author

Dellani Oakes is a former A.P. English teacher and photojournalist. Now working as a substitute teacher and Mary Kay consultant, she can give skin care & makeup advice, correct grammar, take pictures and write an article while controlling a classroom full of rowdy third graders.

Dellani is the author of *Lone Wolf and Indian Summer* and *Ninja Tattoo*. Find her at http://dellanioakes.wordpress.com/ and writersanctuary.blogspot.com

DJ Swerdloff, student

DJ is a freshman at Stetson University in Florida, getting his BA in business and going for a law degree upon graduation.

Donald Riggio, author

Donald Riggio was born and raised in the Bronx, New York and has had a deep and enduring love of rock and roll music since he was a boy. His love of writing is equally enduring as is illustrated in his success as a short story and technical writer over the years.

He combined his two passions with the publication of his first novel, _Seven-Inch Vinyl: A Rock and Roll Novel_, in 2011. That book became a #1 Kindle Best Seller in the music category as did the sequel, _Beyond Vinyl: The Rock and Roll Saga Continues_ published in 2012.

He also hosts a hugely successful Facebook page, where he and his 3,500+ friends discuss, post pictures, rock and roll song links and information 24/7. He invites everyone to join him.

Mr. Riggio lives in Las Vegas, Nevada, where he is currently writing the third book in his trilogy, When Gold Turns to Gray.

Fran Lewis, Author, reviewer, educator, talk show host, creator of _MJ Magazine_

Fran Lewis: Fran worked in the NYC Public Schools as the Reading and Writing Staff Developer for over thirty-six years. She has three masters degrees and a PD in Supervision and Administration. Currently, she is a member of Who's Who of America's Teachers and Who's Who of America's Executives from Cambridge. In addition, she is the author of three children's books and a fourth that has just been published on Alzheimer's disease in order to honor her mom and help create more awareness for a cure. The title of her new Alzheimer's book is _Memories are Precious: Alzheimer's Journey; Ruth's story and Sharp as a Tack and Scrambled Eggs Which Describes Your Brain_? Fran is also the author of _Faces Behind the Stones, Bad Choices_, and M.J. Magazine, an E-Magazine dedicated to the memory of her sister Marcia Joyce. She is also a member of Continental's Who's Who of America's Executives and Professionals and the author of 11 titles. She is presently working on creating a second radio show called Chat Time with Fran Lewis on Blog Talk Radio the Red River Network and adding more outstanding shows on the World of Ink Network. Her show Book Discussion is heard all over the world and she has many listeners.

She was the musical director for shows in her school and ran the school's newspaper. Fran writes reviews for authors upon request and for several other sites. You can read some of her reviews on Ezine.comand on ijustfinished.com under the name Gabina. Here is the link to her radio show www.blogtalkradio.com

Karen Vaughan, author

Karen H. Vaugan is a first-time author who enjoys reading and writing. She is a part of Class 1983 at Applewood Heights Secondary School in Mississauga, ON. She is married with one daughter, and four stepchildren. She has two cats at home. She has a warped sense of humor and sees the lighter side of things.

She is the co-author of _Dead on Arrival_ (Julie Faulkner), _Daytona Dead, Over Her Dead Body,_ and _Dead Comic Standing_. Books may be purchased from her website at www.KarenVaughan.info

Kenneth Weene, author

Life itches and torments Kenneth Weene like pesky flies. Annoyed, he picks up a pile of paper to slap at the buzzing and often whacks himself on the head. Each whack is another story. At least having half-blinded himself, he has learned to not wave the pencil about. Ken will, however, write on until the last gray cell has retreated and there are no longer these strange ideas demanding his feeble efforts. So many poems, stories, novels; and more to come.

Learn more about Ken at http://www.kennethweene.com and find Ken's novels in print, e-format, and audio.

Mark Bouton, author

Mark Bouton writes mystery and nonfiction books. He worked for the FBI and "nabbed killers, kidnappers, and bank robbers." He also played a key role in solving the Oklahoma City bombing. He uses his experiences to inform his writing. His books move fast, with lots of action, humor, strange characters, and striking plot twists.

He has also written a nonfiction book about how to tell when someone's lying. He has learned to read faces, bodies, and voices to avoid being fooled ever again.

John Emil Augustine, author

John Emil Augustine is an author at Master Koda Select Publishing. He toured in his twenties and early thirties with local and national acts; writing, arranging, and performing on the road with well-known Jazz, Blues, Gospel, Reggae, Post Funk, Prog Rock, and Folk Rock groups. John has also been a landscaper, mail carrier, English professor, and forklift operator. He currently lives in Minneapolis, MN with his wife and four boys.

Learn more about him by visiting these websites: http://masterkodaselectpublishing.com and http://www.johnemilaugustine.com

Mark Rubenstein, author

Mark Rubinstein was born in Brooklyn, New York. He dreamed of playing baseball for the Brooklyn Dodgers since his all-time hero was the Dodgers' first baseman Gil Hodges. Rubinstein played high school baseball and ran track. His love of sports led him to read sports fiction, and soon he became a voracious reader, developing an enduring love for all kinds of novels.

He graduated from New York University with a degree in business administration. He then served in the army and ended up as a field medic tending to paratroopers of the 82nd Airborne Division. He was so taken with these experiences that after his discharge, he re-entered NYU as a premed student.

He entered medical school at the State University of New York's Downstate Medical Center. As a medical student, he developed an interest in psychiatry, discovering in that specialty the same thing he realized in reading fiction: every patient has a compelling story to tell. He became a board-certified psychiatrist practicing in New York City.

In addition to running his private practice he developed an interest in forensic psychiatry because the drama and conflict of the cases and courtrooms tapped into his personality style. He also taught psychiatric residents, interns, psychologists, and social workers at New York Presbyterian Hospital and became a clinical assistant professor at Cornell University's medical school.

Before turning to fiction, Rubinstein coauthored five medical self-help books: *The First Encounter: The Beginnings in Psychotherapy* (Jason Aronson); *The Complete Book of Cosmetic Facial Surgery* (Simon and Schuster); *New Choices: the Latest Options in Treating Breast Cancer* (Dodd Mead); *Heartplan: A Complete Program for Total Fitness of Heart & Mind* (McGraw-Hill), and *The Growing Years: A Guide to Your Child's Emotional Development from Birth to Adolescence* (Atheneum).

Rubinstein lives in Connecticut with his wife and as many dogs as she will allow in the house. He still practices psychiatry and is busily writing more novels. *Mad Dog House*, his first novel, was named a Finalist for the 2012 *ForeWord Reviews* Book of the Year Award (Thriller & Suspense).

Martha Cheves, author

Writes cookbooks and *Stir, Laugh, Repeat* is her first book. Her cookbooks are different and use simple recipes with common ingredients found in most kitchens. She says, "No matter how many mistakes you make, never give up. When I was around six years old I talked my mother into letting me make the biscuits for dinner. They came out just a bit hard. In fact they were so hard that my oldest brother hit my youngest brother with one and he ended up with a black eye. Now those were some really BAD biscuits. But I didn't give up and I now make deliciously light and fluffy biscuits that people actually ask for."

Maxine Horton Bringenberg, editor

Maxine Horton Bringenberg was raised in the mountains of northeastern Kentucky, in a little town on the Ohio River, and calls herself a "river rat." The youngest of thirteen children, she holds a special place in her heart for the memories of her youth. Life has allowed her to live in many locations, including Atlanta and Florida's Gulf Coast, but she currently resides in a suburb of Columbus, Ohio with her husband, two grown children, and four cats. Much of her adult life has been spent working with adults with special needs, and also in the health care field. But since childhood, Maxine has had a love of the written word, and a few years ago was delighted to be given the opportunity to edit mostly fictional books. While she has not yet published a book of her own, the authors she works with now are a constant source of inspiration, and she hopes to find her muse soon.

R.J. Ellory, Best selling author

R.J. Ellory is the author of *Three Days in Chicagoland*, which focuses on the brutal murder of a young girl in Chicago in 1956, as told from three different viewpoints: The Sister, The Cop and The Killer. His other books are *Candlemoth, Ghostheart, A Quiet Vendetta, City of Lies, A Quiet Belief in Angels, A Simple*

Act of Violence, The Anniversary Man, Saints of New York, Bad Signs, A Dark and Broken Heart, The Devil and the River. Visit his website: *www.RJEllory.com*

Robin Surface

Robin Surface is president of Fideli Publishing Inc., and an avid reader and supporter of independent authors and their books. She reads 250-300 books per year and almost all of them are by independent, self-published and small press titles. Her professional goal is to help authors create the best books possible.

Susan Ross, Children's Book Reviewer

Susan is a former school secretary who worked over twenty years in the New York City Public School System. She is an avid reader and enjoys reading to her three grandchildren. Her main goal is to encourage young children to read many different types of books. Susan's reviews will hopefully encourage parents and young children to read more and choose some of the books that she spotlighted as her best picks in this issue.

Trish Jackson, author

Trish writes emotive romantic suspense focusing on small towns, country folk and their animals. *www.trishjax.com*

CHECK BACK AT YOUR FAVORITE E-RETAILER FOR NEW EDITIONS EVERY OTHER MONTH!

I hope you enjoy reading, and we encourage comments and contributors.

- To be considered for a position as one of MJ Magazine's book reviewers, please contact Fran at riffyone@optonline.net and use **I'd like to be an MJ Magazine book reviewer** as your subject line.

- If you would like to contribute an article, please send the article, a photograph of yourself in .jpg format and a short bio using the subject line **Article for MJ Magazine** to Fran at riffyone@optonline.net (sending a submission does not guarantee it will be run).

- If you would like to have your book reviewed by *MJ Magazine*, please contact Fran (riffyone@optonline.net) for information about eligibility, requirements and mailing information using the subject line **MJ Magazine Book Review Information.**

- Tell us what you think about our first issue, what you'd like to see in subsequent issues, etc. by emailing riffyone@optonline.net with the subject line **Comments for MJ Magazine.**

Until next time …

www.ingramcontent.com/pod-product-compliance
Lightning Source LLC
Chambersburg PA
CBHW080251030426
42334CB00023BA/2782